• Distributed by Big O Publishing Limited, 219 Eversleigh Road, London SW11 5UY Telephone 01-228 3392 Telex 914549 • Cover illustration by Jim Burns • Back cover illustration by Brian Lewis • Title logo— ©1978—George Snow • Book designed by George Snow • •Technical information provided by Jim Burns, Brian Lewis & Saul Dunn • Printed and bound in Hong Kong by Mandarin Offset Ltd • First published in Great Britain in 1978. PIERROT PUBLISHING LIMITED, London • Text— ©Harry Harrison 1978 • All rights reserved. No part of this publication may be reproduced in any form or by any means without prior permission in writing from Pierrot Publishing Limited or the various original copyright holders. • ISBN 0 905310 21 7 • This is an Intergalactic Space Command volume and all enquiries regarding its contents should be addressed to ISC Publications Inc., 44989, Delta Avenue, Achamandura City, Achamandura, Sinian System • Designoids Catherine Denvir and Kevin Klone-Sparrow • Compugraphic typesetting Nik Lumsden.

HARRY HARRISON

# CONTENTS

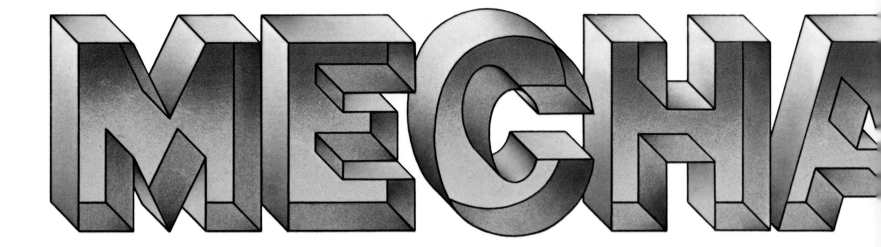

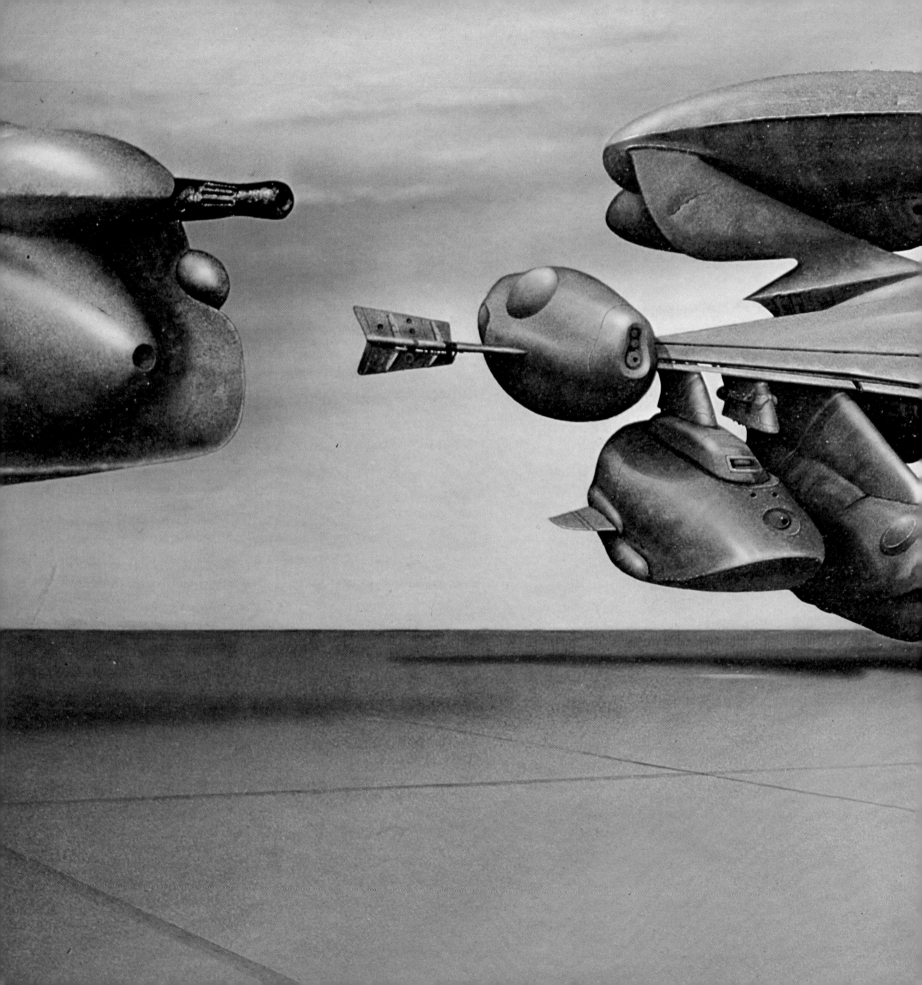

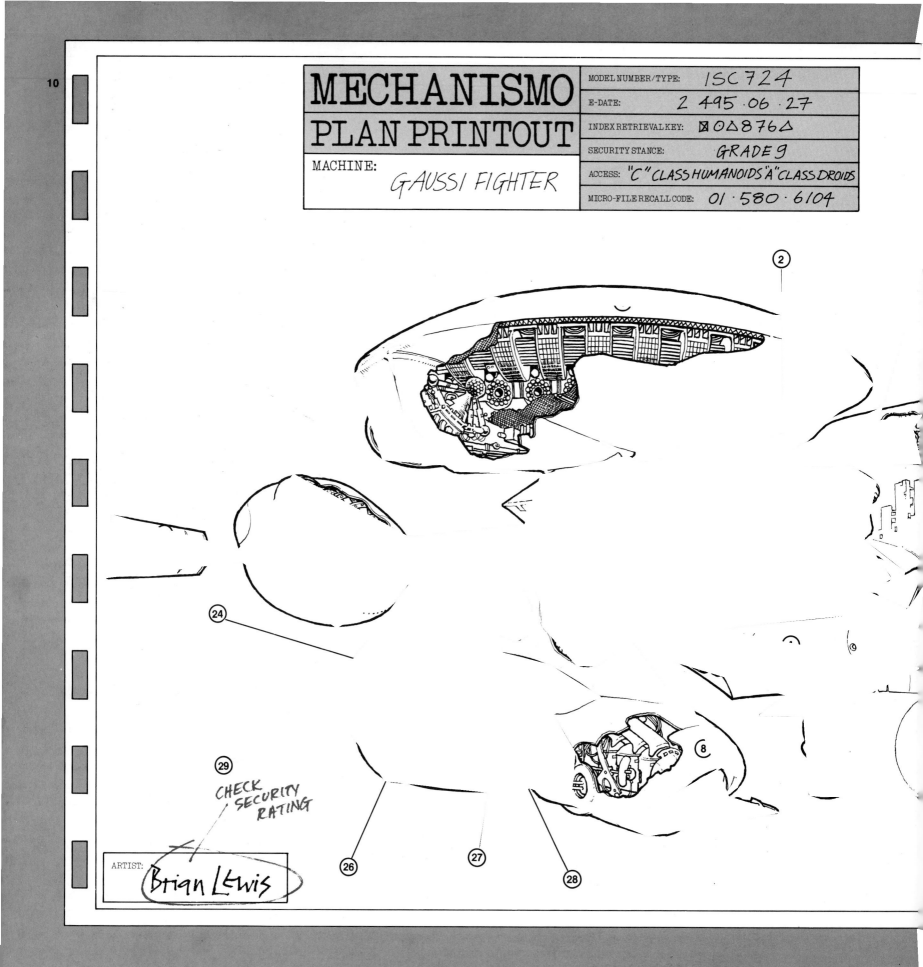

# MECHANISMO
# PLAN PRINTOUT

MACHINE: *GAUSSI FIGHTER*

| | |
|---|---|
| MODEL NUMBER/TYPE: | ISC 724 |
| E-DATE: | 2 495 · 06 · 27 |
| INDEX RETRIEVAL KEY: | ⊠ O △ 8 7 6 △ |
| SECURITY STANCE: | GRADE 9 |
| ACCESS: | "C" CLASS HUMANOIDS "A" CLASS DROIDS |
| MICRO-FILE RECALL CODE: | 01 · 580 · 6104 |

CHECK SECURITY RATING

ARTIST: Brian Lewis

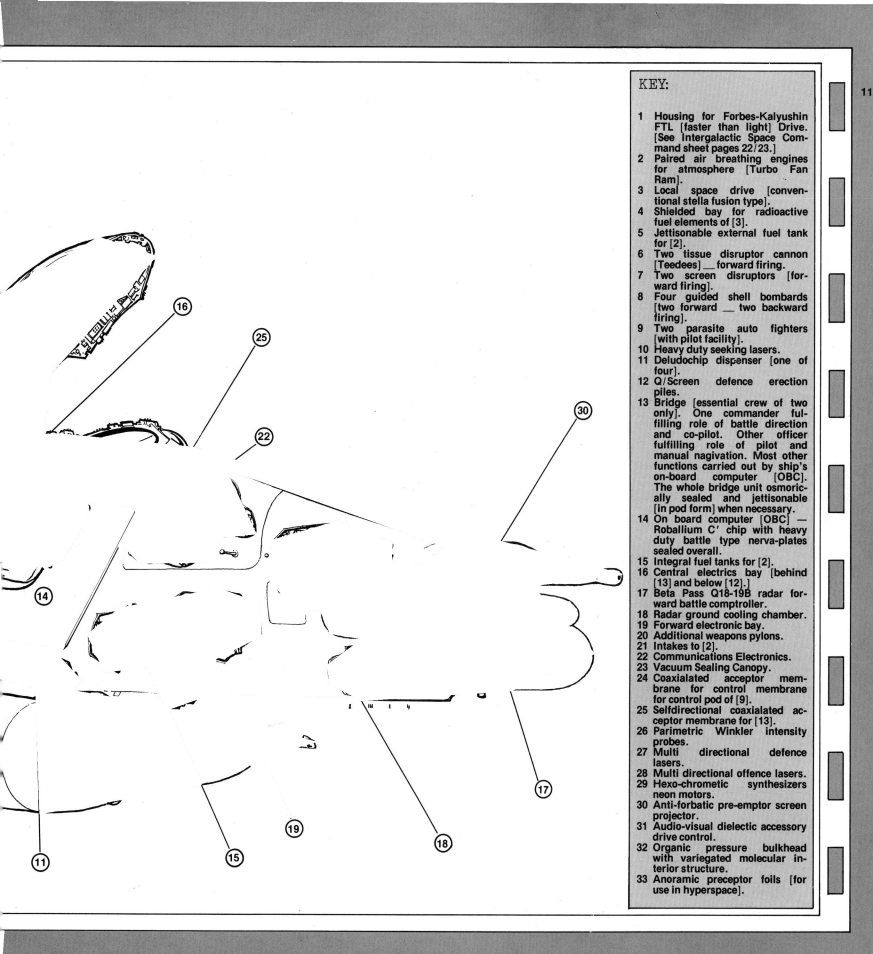

KEY:

1 Housing for Forbes-Kalyushin FTL [faster than light] Drive. [See Intergalactic Space Command sheet pages 22/23.]
2 Paired air breathing engines for atmosphere [Turbo Fan Ram].
3 Local space drive [conventional stella fusion type].
4 Shielded bay for radioactive fuel elements of [3].
5 Jettisonable external fuel tank for [2].
6 Two tissue disruptor cannon [Teedees] __ forward firing.
7 Two screen disruptors [forward firing].
8 Four guided shell bombards [two forward __ two backward firing].
9 Two parasite auto fighters [with pilot facility].
10 Heavy duty seeking lasers.
11 Deludochip dispenser [one of four].
12 Q/Screen defence erection piles.
13 Bridge [essential crew of two only]. One commander fulfilling role of battle direction and co-pilot. Other officer fulfilling role of pilot and manual nagivation. Most other functions carried out by ship's on-board computer [OBC]. The whole bridge unit osmorically sealed and jettisonable [in pod form] when necessary.
14 On board computer [OBC] — Roballium C' chip with heavy duty battle type nerva-plates sealed overall.
15 Integral fuel tanks for [2].
16 Central electrics bay [behind [13] and below [12].]
17 Beta Pass Q18-19B radar forward battle comptroller.
18 Radar ground cooling chamber.
19 Forward electronic bay.
20 Additional weapons pylons.
21 Intakes to [2].
22 Communications Electronics.
23 Vacuum Sealing Canopy.
24 Coaxialated acceptor membrane for control membrane for control pod of [9].
25 Selfdirectional coaxialated acceptor membrane for [13].
26 Parimetric Winkler intensity probes.
27 Multi directional defence lasers.
28 Multi directional offence lasers.
29 Hexo-chrometic synthesizers neon motors.
30 Anti-forbatic pre-emptor screen projector.
31 Audio-visual dielectic accessory drive control.
32 Organic pressure bulkhead with variegated molecular interior structure.
33 Anoramic preceptor foils [for use in hyperspace].

# MECHANISMO-FILE PRINTOUT

| | | |
|---|---|---|
| TITLE: | FACT SHEET - GAUSSI FIGHTER ("LITTLE NELL") ISC 724 | E-DATE: 2495.06.27 |
| | | INDEX RETRIEVAL KEY: ☐△O2.13☒ |

| | | | | | |
|---|---|---|---|---|---|
| SECURITY STANCE: GRADE 6 | ACCESS: "A" CLASS HUMANOIDS | SHEET NUMBER: 1 | TOTAL: 1 | SHEETS |
| DUPLICATION: 5 COPIES | THIS COPY NUMBER: 3 | ASSIGNED TO: SAUL DUNN | MICRO-FILE RECALL CODE: 01.370.3524 |

The fiercely fought Division Wars of the late 25th Century saw the development of a great variety of warcraft through the efforts of the combatants involved in the conflict. The Division itself saw the Empire effectively split down the middle, but whilst the Sirius Axis with its desire to return to the status quo continued to equip its many and diverse outposts with standard empire equipment, the opposing Capellan Shards were forced by virtue of their scattered disposition through the Quadrant and their comparatively poor state of military readiness at the onset of the Division to launch whole new programmes of warcraft manufacture (see pages 22/23 for complete ISC sheet).

Most of the Shard systems were compelled either by lack of manufacturing facilities or manpower, or both, to convert civil craft to war use, and in general these found themselves out-gunned in most confrontations with Axis ships. But in a few of the more developed systems types of craft appeared which eventually surpassed the Axis vessels in terms of manoeuvrability, firepower, damage sustaining capacity— in fact in all those areas which delineate equipment effectiveness.

And best of all the craft of the Division Wars, at least in the BAVS (Battle Area Vehicle Supremacy) role was the Gaussi Fighter. This craft first flew on March 2nd 2487 from its home base of Gaussi P10037 in the Capella system, and marked a quantum jump in warcraft design.

Its supremacy over any of the Axis ships was proven time and time again in 2517 direct ship to ship conflicts, in which the Gaussis were credited with 2280 wins, Axis ships with 129 wins, and 108 conflicts were declared indeterminate in outcome. Moreover, this superiority was extended to INATMO Dogfights, as the Gaussi was the only fighter in any of the powers to be built to carry out its BAVS role in both atmosphere and deep space. It is this diversity of functions which gives the Gaussi its particular appearance— a deceptive one, for behind the apparent quaintness of design lurks an immensely formidable craft.

The colour illustration on the previous pages shows the Gaussi 724 (known to her crews as 'Little Nell') undergoing routine servicing at the Antigrav yards on Gaussi P10037 after her legendary encounter with a flight of eight Axis 'Hero-Class' deep space frigates, latest design. Herself absorbing only minimal damage 'Little Nell' rendered four of the enemy radioactive dust, crippled one other, whilst the remaining three wisely flicked into sub-space and fled to safety.

Full travel and armament capacities of the Gaussi 724 may be found in the Intergalactic Space Command Sheet on pages 22/23.

*"She's forty seconds late again—ought to take the old cheesebox off the line."*

**M**ANKIND'S DESIRE to leave the Earth and get out there and explore the heavenly bodies was a fond subject for many authors well before the advent of science fiction. As early as 1638 Francis Godwin sent his voyager on his way in *Man in the Moon* on a raft pulled by great birds, a trip made theoretically possible by the Earth and the Moon sharing the same atmosphere. Cyrano's flying chariot makes its *Voyage dans la Lune* a few years later in 1650 using a series of novel means of propulsion. The first flight is attempted with vials of dew which, sucked up by the sun, lift the chariot. It doesn't get very far. After trying a large spring, then rockets—opportunity missed here!—he finally succeeds in reaching the Moon through the powers of beef marrow to ''draw'' him there, just as the marrow draws out an inflammation. Pretty simple stuff and more related to the fantasy of flying carpets than scientific propulsion. Even the slightest trace of logic had to wait until 1865 when Jules Verne got his travellers *From the Earth to the Moon* in a shell fired from a large gun. Verne had only the dimmest knowledge of natural science—he lifted his ideas from texts of science and pseudo-science with equal enthusiasm—so he never realised that not only would his characters be pulped to a thin layer of jelly, but that his vehicle would be crushed flat as well. The fired-from-a-gun idea was picked up again by H.G. Wells in 1936 for the film *Things to Come*. Wells improved the design slightly by having multiple barrels within the gun, one firing after the other to give continuous acceleration. (Though I have always wondered why the barrels themselves didn't go shooting out of the cannon to crash down onto the landscape.) Earlier, in 1901, Wells had dodged around the propulsion problem by getting *The First Men in the Moon* on their way in a ship lifted by Cavorite, a miraculous material that acts as a gravity insulator.

It wasn't until the 1920's when the theories of rocket flight were actually put to practical use that the idea of rocket propulsion entered fiction. The first craft were usually built in the back garden by giften amateurs who gave long lectures on rocketry, cribbed from scientific journals. The story ended when the rocket craft took off. There was obviously room for improvement in plot, as well as machines, and this period passed in a flash and rockets took their proper place as the accepted mode of space transportation. The first SF pulps were filled with them, blasting, rattling and roaring into the sky. They were fuelled with ''fuel'', and it was only the most daring author who was more specific than that. (Though I remember fondly one gasoline-powered ship.)

If the writers were shy with descriptions the artists were not, and wonderful were the vehicles to behold. Frank R. Paul, the master of SF art, was the most inventive and talented of the lot. He never repeated a design and went well beyond the usual smooth, flying phalluses. His ships were blistered, ported, convoluted and utterly fascinating. Spaceship design rested with him until the eccentric flying collections of bric-a-brac of *2001* came along. Today with professional designers in the act, we get the kinky constructs of *Star Wars*, so much more interesting than conventional designs like Soyuz and Apollo.

Giantism in spaceship design was on the scene pretty early, since an author can type *one mile* as easily as he can *one foot*. So the battlecraft described by E.E. Smith and John W. Campbell, Jr. were a mile long and were wondrous to behold. Particularly when they were sliced in half by ravening rays so the occupants could fall out of the severed ends and scream and explode in space and have other interesting things happen to them. Large size was of course essential to the generation ship, the simplest— though not the most reliable—way to reach the stars. The idea was basic enough; build a spaceship big enough to contain a complete ecology of its own. Everything would be recycled through plants, animals, and machinery, and as long as you were putting energy into the system people could live in the ship forever. Of course it would take some years to reach the stars and the original crew would never live to see their destination. But later generations of their descendants would—hence the name generation ships. The only thing really wrong with these ships was the plot line. There is nothing more boring than a 200-year journey where nothing happens. So, traditionally, the generation ships break down and it is the rare story where one of them gets through unscathed.

But the generation ships went the way of rockets and sail when the FTL craft burst through the ether. Faster Than Light. Of course Dr. Einstein has told us that this is impossible. We can get close to the speed of light, his theory states, but never equal or pass it. This light barrier is not as easy to penetrate as the sound barrier. (Though it has been done. I recall one creaking story, read in my youth, where the ship does go faster than the traditional limit of 186,282.397 miles a second, whereupon the pinhead pilot smiles his idiot's grin and says, "Guess it looks like Einstein was wrong!") The answer seems to be that if you cannot break the barrier of the speed of light you can always go around it. Many and fascinating are the descriptions of how this works. The fourth dimension comes in handy here. If you imagine three-dimensional space as a piece of paper, normal travel is across the surface of the paper. However if you fold the sheet of paper back upon itself you can pass from one place on the surface to another through the "fourth dimension". Sounds good—and sure keeps the story moving. So the chemical rockets are replaced, or assisted, by the new "drive". Invariably a sealed case with heavy cables running to it. So when the button is pressed the spaceship goes into jumpspace or warpspace or overdrive or

CAPTION:
**PAGES 16/17**

TITLE:
**GAUSSI PFCV 14**

The craft illustrated on the following pages was developed during the Division Wars as a Personal Flight Command Vehicle (PFCV) used largely by the Space vice-Marshalls involved in the tactical efforts against the Axis craft. Its full capacities and specifications are outlined in the ISC sheet on pages 22/23. It was largely used by Space vice-Marshall Talian, a legendary figure, responsible for most of the thrusts into Axis territories, and instrumental in spearheading the most successful BAVS (Battle Area Vehicle Supremacy) roles. Space vice-Marshall Talian may be seen on a foray into Earth's solar system, working with the crew of the 'Transolar' in the intergalactic space port of Janus, a moon in orbit about Saturn (pages 48/49, figure on extreme right). Additional information surrounding his role within the Capellan forces may be found on pages 50/51.
The Gaussi PFCV 14 is seen on the following pages (16/17) in transit from Achamandura, about to land on the Central Command Port of Gaussi P10037.

some other kind of star drive, and with a zip is somewhere else instantly. E.E. Smith was one of the first with his inertialess drive, another magic diddling with the laws of physics, simply one more excuse to get us to the stars quickly so that the story can proceed.

Most of the language of spaceships takes the sea as its source. We can talk of decks and bulkheads, galleys, and even engine rooms and get a feeling of security. (Made even more homely in A. Bertram Chandler's Rim Runner books where the spacecraft really are ocean-going vessels in space. The author, a ship's master, knows what he is doing.) This is particularly true of space warfare where the space Navy is just that. The preposterous idea that we can take war into space has launched a million SF battleships, and is so expensively attractive to the military mind that much money is actually being spent today on research to this end. This practice is enthusiastically encouraged by hysterical articles about "bombs in orbit" and "Rays from space". Both the Generals, and the journalists, forget that it takes as much energy to get a bomb down from orbit as it does to get it up. While the inflexible ordering of the Law of Inverse Squares dictates that at orbital distances laser beams, or rays of any kind, are about as lethal as a car's headlight. The law states that the energy content of any form of radiation decreases by the inverse square of the distance. Or, to put it in slightly more simple form, radiation goes out equally in all directions so that the amount received at any one point in the constantly expanding sphere of propagation is going to be a helluva lot less than it was at the single point source.

But logic cannot argue with all of the fiction on the subject, including super moneymaker *Star Wars*, so we can expect more not less space battles. And the ships that fight these battles will have to be equipped with better means of propulsion than chemical fuels.

That's all we have now; liquid and solid fuels that burn, to expand, to generate thrust. But far more interesting ideas are on the scientific drawing boards and slipping into the SF stories. Atomic drives are being developed, even one that uses a series of atomic explosions for thrust. There is also a space scoop with a big maw to suck in the debris of space—estimated at one molecule the cubic metre—to use as energy and material for thrust. Even the power of light has been considered, the pressure of photons on miles-square thin sails, used dramatically in Clarke's *The Wind from the Sun* ■

# MECHANISMO-FILE PRINTOUT

TITLE: **INTERGALACTIC SPACE COMMAND**

E-DATE: 2526.05.16
INDEX RETRIEVAL KEY: 0△0749 ☒

SECURITY STANCE: INTELLIGENT DROIDS
ACCESS: DISCRETIONARY
SHEET NUMBER: 1
TOTAL: 2 SHEETS

DUPLICATION: 6 COPIES
THIS COPY NUMBER: 2
ASSIGNED TO: K. JACOBS
MICRO-FILE RECALL CODE: 01.486 7389

## SPACE/ORBITAL/ATMOSPHERE GROUND TO AIR/SPACE TRANSPORT

### Gaussi Fighter 724

BAVS Equipment —

*Dimensions:*
Span—107.25 metres
Length—98.3 metres
Height—23.75 metres
Weight—1,260,000K (empty)
1,980,500K (full battle trim)
2,200,000K (max. overload)

*Performance:* Max speed 'INATMO':
3,750 knots (on air breathers)
4,500 knots (with governed local space drive augmentor)
Max speed 'EXATMO':
12.50 DBVU (750,000 knots surface relative)
13.95 DBVU (930,000 knots S.R. with auto-rational red de-governing)

*Standard provision for sub-space FTL flight.*

*Armament:*
[*offensive*]
1. Paired forward screen disruptors of up to 85,000 Q/therms capacity.
2. Paired forward 'Teedees' (Tissue disrupt ion cannon)
3. 10 heavy duty seeking-lasers (for strike role)
4. 4 conventional guided shell bombards with 1500 rounds each.

[*defensive*]
1. A variety of external defences but typically: 2 parasite auto-fighters of limitless 'G' manoeuvrability capacity.
2. 4 local space 'Deludochips'

*Armour:*
1. Standard battle-gauge Q/screen defence
2. Outline dazzle projectors
3. Hull plating on 85% of outer skin 8mm synthacarborillidium
4. Quintuple redundant wall and bulkhead clever metal repair capacity.

10817 fighters of the Gaussi type were build in the 35 standard years of the Divison conflict and it is a comment on the genius of the original design that no significant changes were made right through the production run. The longest serving vessel of the type was No.2638 (MAE WEST) which was recommissioned into service with the Capella Based New Empire at the termination of hostilities, given a coat of white paint and remained in active front line service for 172 standard years until her clever metal self repair facilities had changed her aerodynamic form so much that she had become virtually unflyable INATMO. She was relegated to minor deep-space duties and continued to give faithful service until a 7 billion tonne rogue asteroid overloaded her self repair capabilities.

### Gaussi PFCV 14

Standard Equipment—

*Dimensions:*
Span—94.38 metres
Length—73.20 metres
Height—31.50 metres (rear tail height)
Weight—400,480K (empty)
427,560K (full personnel)
500,100K (max. overload)

*Performance:* Max speed 'INATMO':
2,500 knots (air breathers)
3,400 knots (GLSDA)
Max speed 'EXATMO':

13.95 (930,000 knots S.R.)
(DBVU) 15.20 (special Ex-boost speed facilities)

*Long distance FTL hyperspace facilities for use in case of pursuit.*

*Armament:*
1. Forward screen cannon disruptors of up to 92,000 Q/therm capacity
2. Four heavy duty proton cannon at front and rear of hull
3. Two light duty manoeuvrability proton cannon on each wing

*Armour:*
1. Standard Q/screen defence
2. Heat haze disturbance vectors
3. De-molecular variance projectors
4. Clever metal repair facilities

The PFCV 14 was largely a senior personnel carrier as described on page 15, and its prime function was to be able to travel fast and lose any aggressors that might attack. It was therefore built for long space/time jumps and its maximum EXATMO speed could be achieved at massive thrust, from base 2,500 knots to 15.20 DBVU in a minimum of 14 seconds, a record in space speed flight.

## Hyper-space Troop Carrier. Barns HTC 9869

*Dimensions:*
Span—No wing span
Length—4440 metres
Height—1232 metres
Weight—272,000,000K (empty)
2,340,000,000K (max freight and personnel capacity)

*Performance:* Max speed 'Exatmo' 4.23 DBVU (S.R.)

*Light speed facilities available but build requirements state 4 hours (S.R.) to break into Hyperspace.*

The HTC 9869 was built purely for intergalactic heavy personnel transfers, carrying up to 2 million people at one time. It never landed from the date it was built to the date it was blown out of space (with some 900,000 people aboard) by a fleet of renegade space pirates who fired a freak proton torpedo at the hyper drive pile which exploded and dematerialised the entire craft.

## MISC. SPACE COMMAND FEATURES

**Cybernetics:** Battle Robot BMU 657
*Dimensions:*
Height—134 metres
Girth—40.20 metres
Weight—1,339,000K (empty)
1,834,000K (fully armed)

*Armaments:*
1. 18 anti-ballistic hydronic warhead missile tubes, with standard ammunition facility of 122 missiles on board
2. 8 forward tissue disruptors (Teedee cannon)
3. 9 rear tissue disruptors
4. Four proton cannon
5. 54 heavy duty seeking lasers
6. 32 guided shell bombards
7. 2 'white-heat' stream lasers with 'curtain' strike facility
8. 8 conventional hyper-therm burners
9. 324 light duty 'spot-lasers' with cutting capacity of 44 milli-morts per second

**Chronomics:** Paterson TD 45
*Dimensions:*
In-space diameter: 320.00 metres
In-space height: 210.34 metres (dome top)
*Performance:* Time Dilatation Capacity:
24 Ch Dr's per h. rel.
(Auto-anti-warp pace) 31 ChDr's per H. rel.
Maximum non-correctable TD: 445 tone seconds

## DEFINITIONS

**BAVS** — Battle Area Vehicle Supremacy.
**INATMO** — In atmosphere performance.
**EXATMO** — Outside atmosphere performance (e.g. a photon drive space launch could not perform INATMO and neither could a craft of greater than 400 metres length.
**DVBU** — Speed measurement relating to sub-light speed travel.
**Clever metal** — a form of auto-repair system developed on Earth in the late 20th century in which metal 'grows' and therefore repairs itself.

# MECHAN.

ONE OF THE DANGERS that haunts the SF pages is the looming form of the threatening robot. The earliest of these were constructed of flesh and bone, what would now be called androids; Frankenstein's monster (1817) and Capek's *R.U.R.*, (1923), Rossum's Universal Robots, the source of the term. The idea that if you built it it couldn't be good carries on through C.C. Campbell's ''The Avatar'' (1935) where the perfect artificial man becomes dictator of the world and has to be destroyed.

It was only with the construction of metal robots—obedient machines that mechanical men began operating on the side of justice. In the early pulp magazine, Frank Reade's Steam Man fought the Indians for the good guys, and Eando Binder's robot, built for peace to prove its worth to mankind, was smart enough to choose sides against the Nazis in ''Adam Link Fights a War''. Edmond Hamilton's Captain Future could count upon the faithful robot, Krag, to aid him at all times, as well as the faithful but not so nice android, Lothar.

A later development is the part man, part metal (or plastic) creature. This theme, and the psychological effects of the additions, has been explored successfully in Budrys's *Who* (1958), and more recently in the preposterous TV bionic man, woman, dog, hamster, etc. series. The authors of these stories never seem to have realised that all mechanical substitutes for human parts are far weaker than the originals; the bionic man needs a wheelchair—not a springboard to leap over buildings. We must slip far into the future to rationalise a superior technology to make the creature work well, as in Saul Dunn's *Mandroid*, who is only ten per cent human, the rest being manufactured parts.

A touch of order entered robotic circles in 1940 with Asimov's ''Robby'' and ''Liar''. The mechanical men now began to clank about radiating security, since they had the Laws of Robotics stamped into their positronic brains. Asimov gets full credit for these laws, and countless are the writers who have utilised them:

1. A robot may not injure a human being, or, through inaction, allow a a human being to come to harm.
2. A robot must obey the orders given it by human beings except where such orders would conflict with the First Law.
3. A robot must protect its own existence as long as such protection does not conflict with the First or Second Law.

Once the robotic threat had been removed the infinitely varied relationships of robot to man could be explored. Clifford Simak, in his *City* series, shows mankind evolving and leaving the Earth to the robots and highly evolved dogs. Jack Williamson's *With Folded Hands . . .* (1947) does discover a danger in robot control, but a benevolent one. To prevent men

CAPTION:

PAGES 32/33

TITLE:

BMU 657

The majority of land arms used in the Division Wars during the 25th century consisted of massive perambulatory battle robots known as BMU's. These robots conducted all spearhead attacks, and infantry drives within Axis territories and were landed upon the planets by massive transport freighters such as the 'Transolar' (featured on pages 50 /51). They were controlled from internal crew pods situated in the head section which carried independent flight facilities in case of robot destruction. The crew, in general, numbered 120 members with computer sections and armaments sections positioned in the central chest area of the machine.

Full capacities and specifications are featured in the ISC sheets on pages 22/23.

from being hurt the robots are stunting all development of the human race. With all the robotic goodness around it was a pleasure to see Alfred Bester's "Fondly Fahrenheit" about a slightly insane robot.

Having once assigned man's attribute to a machine, we must consider the relationship of this intelligent machine to man's mystical nature. Boucher's "The Quest for Saint Aquin" asks if it is possible to have a robot saint? Silverberg answered the question years later with "Good News from the Vatican". If you can have a robot Pope—then why not a saint?

Robots are seen as part and parcel of mankind's existence, even in the marketplace. Pohl's "Tunnel Under the World" (1954) has unsuspecting little robots running a continuous market survey, which logically leads into his "Midas Plague" (1954) where they solve a robot-created marketing problem.

Of course these are just the human-appearing robots, although there is no good reason at all to shape a robot in this manner, other than it looks nice and they are handy to have around the house. Real robots, the ones actually in use in industry today, look nothing at all like the classic clanker. The commonest are just collections of machine tools and mechanical manipulators. You can actually watch them work and not realise for a bit that the grey box to the side is controlling things, not a human operator.

SF also has non-humanoid robots of this kind. The computer controlled fully automated spaceship has been with us for quite a while. In the Old Doc Methuselah series by L. Ron Hubbard—disguised behind the pen-name of Rene Lafayette—the robot ship is the second stock character after doc. Fully automated cities have had their day, usually so well designed that they keep operating after their inhabitants are gone, and fully automated trains ran first in the pages of science fiction. (They run in reality now in the Dallas-Fort Worth airport. It is a little disconcerting to sit alone in a small car, without a driver, while the thing whistles and clatters through the track complex. They also have a high failure rate which makes the owners wish that they had kept Casey Jones at the throttle.) At sea we have Bass's *Godwhale*, a sentient giant robot designed for harvesting plankton for undersea food processing plants. In space—and at war again—are Saberhagen's Berserkers, super war machines, launched by alien nutters, whose job it is to zip about the galaxy destroying all forms of life■

*We must turn Jepson in for a new model. It's the third time this week that he's dropped the soup and his calorie counter hasn't registered right since Easter.*

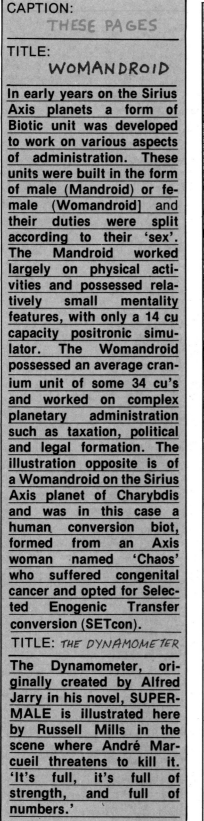

CAPTION:
THESE PAGES

TITLE:

## WOMANDROID

In early years on the Sirius Axis planets a form of Biotic unit was developed to work on various aspects of administration. These units were built in the form of male (Mandroid) or female (Womandroid] and their duties were split according to their 'sex'. The Mandroid worked largely on physical activities and possessed relatively small mentality features, with only a 14 cu capacity positronic simulator. The Womandroid possessed an average cranium unit of some 34 cu's and worked on complex planetary administration such as taxation, political and legal formation. The illustration opposite is of a Womandroid on the Sirius Axis planet of Charybdis and was in this case a human conversion biot, formed from an Axis woman named 'Chaos' who suffered congenital cancer and opted for Selected Enogenic Transfer conversion (SETcon).

TITLE: *THE DYNAMOMETER*

The Dynamometer, originally created by Alfred Jarry in his novel, SUPER-MALE is illustrated here by Russell Mills in the scene where André Marcueil threatens to kill it. 'It's full, it's full of strength, and full of numbers.'

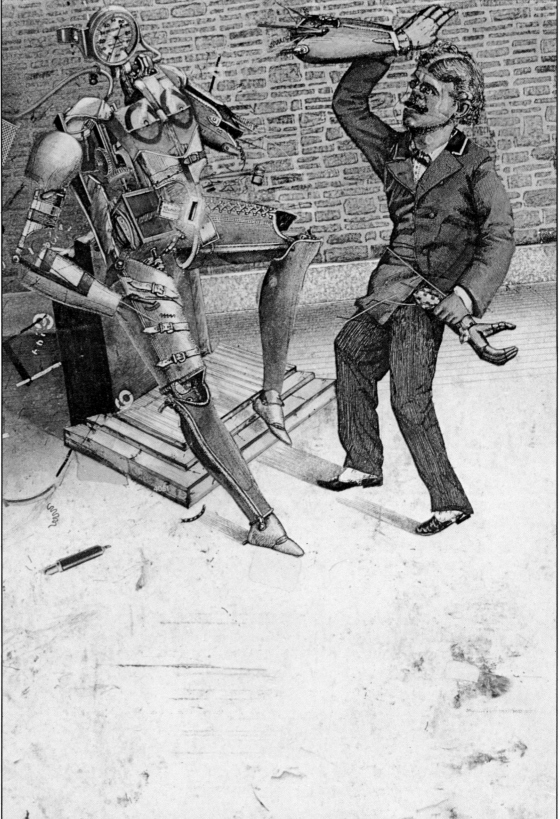

TITLE: ROBOTS LIST

E-DATE: 2525.03.14

INDEX RETRIEVAL KEY: O⊠△694⊠

SECURITY STANCE: NONE    ACCESS: GENERAL    SHEET NUMBER: 1    TOTAL: 1 SHEETS

DUPLICATION: U/L   COPIES   THIS COPY NUMBER: /    ASSIGNED TO: MR. LEWIS    MICRO-FILE RECALL CODE: 01.267.0053

**1. PSEUDO-CYBORG.** The most advanced robot-type ever developed; capable of advanced self-perpetuating thought, mental capacities far advanced beyond man, special mathematical capabilities, used for legal arbitration, complex accounting administration and high posts in industry. Developed by Sirius Axis planets. Built from skin and flesh cultures, organic transplants and 'clever metal' bone structures. (For technical details of clever metal — see ISC sheet — pages 22/23. For visual example see page 48, 2nd left.)

**2. MANDROID/WOMANDROID.** Generally used for administration (see page 37) duties on Sirius Axis planets when first developed but later becoming alternative human form on Charybdis. Android form, all non-human capacities, average useful span — 300 years.

**3. CYBORG.** Tactical infantry unit, used both in hand-to-hand battle requirements and espionage requirements. Base human form, but entirely Biotic build, with clever metal skin and electronic relay units, positronic brain facilities, limited mental abilities but huge physical strength. Developed by Gaussi planets for tactical efforts in Division Wars.

Special features: Long distance audio units; high capacity viseo range; 300 watt voice output unit; multiple-muscle powered limb units for high speed perambulation.

**4. BIOT.** Essentially a guard robot used largely in space port vicinities where noisome and noxious fuel vapours prove injurious to human guards. Equipped with special 'third eye' feature comprising sixth sense [scientifically explained through extra-sensory perception waves] situated in forehead area behind eyes. Carries either dummy disruptor if used in human contact areas or fully armed disruptor in wartime where first law robotics is cancelled. Highly developed and sensitive robot. Otherwise known as IM4Pd Sentry Biot, developed by the Capellan Shards and built largely from clever metal. They were sometimes nicknamed 'Spooks' because of their appearance (see pages 9 and 39) and were the first Mechs to use lab-grown quasi-human brain analogues for general motor and sensory functions, though logic and memory functions were performed by standard Koballium - C chip modules.

**5. CYBEROID.** A worker robot used mostly in the Capellan territories for farming duties and heavy duty shifting work in wide rural areas. Generally self-controlling but with very limited mental faculties and requiring adjustments for different functions.

**6. BATTLE ROBOTS.** These cybernetic devices have been used by most civilisations involved in interplanetary or intergalactic wars. They can vary according to the requirements and one example of the larger battle robot may be found in the ISC sheets on pages 22/23. Generally they were lethal weaponry robots carrying as many as fifty different armaments with massive speed capabilities.

**7. ANIMOID.** A generic development applied to many different pseudo-animal forms, used for a variety of purposes from guard dog duties to pets on planets where animals have become extinct. On some Capellan Shard planets of slow development the Animoid often took the form of a horse and was used in inter-camp fracas.

# MECHANISMO PLAN PRINTOUT

**MACHINE:** SENTRY BIOT

| | |
|---|---|
| MODEL NUMBER/TYPE: | 1M4Pd |
| E-DATE: | 2525.10.16 |
| INDEX RETRIEVAL KEY: | □ □ △ 743 ☒ |
| SECURITY STANCE: | NONE |
| ACCESS: | GENERAL |
| MICRO-FILE RECALL CODE: | 01.226.0573 |

ARTIST: Brian Lewis

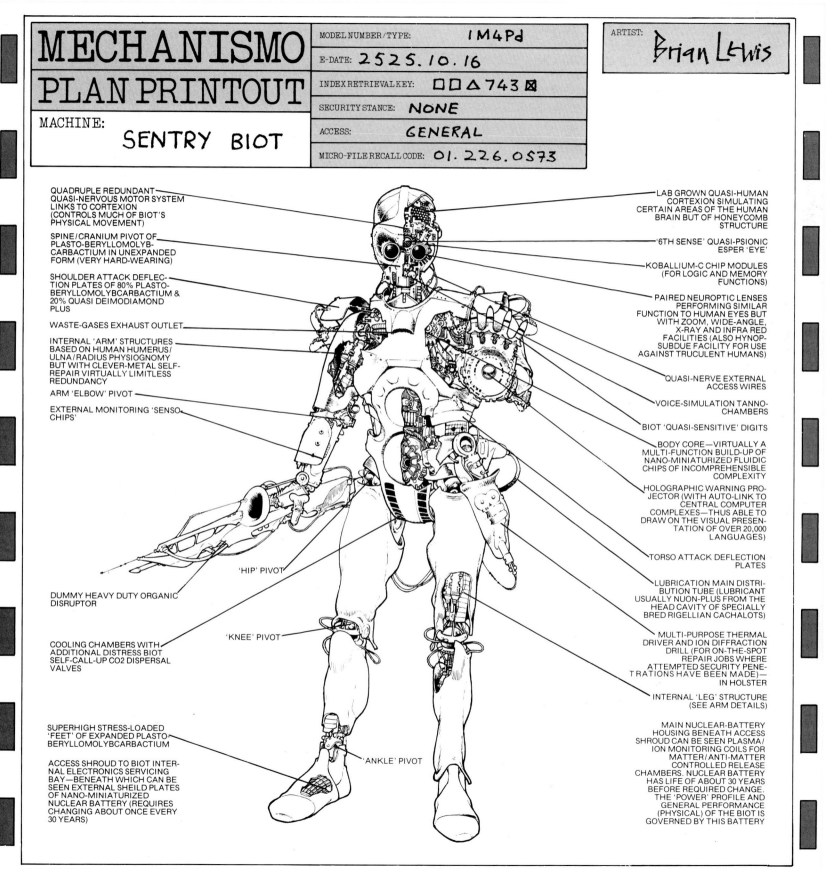

QUADRUPLE REDUNDANT QUASI-NERVOUS MOTOR SYSTEM LINKS TO CORTEXION (CONTROLS MUCH OF BIOT'S PHYSICAL MOVEMENT)

SPINE/CRANIUM PIVOT OF PLASTO-BERYLLOMOLYB-CARBACTIUM IN UNEXPANDED FORM (VERY HARD-WEARING)

SHOULDER ATTACK DEFLEC-TION PLATES OF 80% PLASTO-BERYLLOMOLYBCARBACTIUM & 20% QUASI DEIMODIAMOND PLUS

WASTE-GASES EXHAUST OUTLET

INTERNAL 'ARM' STRUCTURES BASED ON HUMAN HUMERUS/ULNA/RADIUS PHYSIOGNOMY BUT WITH CLEVER-METAL SELF-REPAIR VIRTUALLY LIMITLESS REDUNDANCY

ARM 'ELBOW' PIVOT

EXTERNAL MONITORING 'SENSO CHIPS'

DUMMY HEAVY DUTY ORGANIC DISRUPTOR

COOLING CHAMBERS WITH ADDITIONAL DISTRESS BIOT SELF-CALL-UP CO2 DISPERSAL VALVES

SUPERHIGH STRESS-LOADED 'FEET' OF EXPANDED PLASTO-BERYLLOMOLYBCARBACTIUM

ACCESS SHROUD TO BIOT INTER-NAL ELECTRONICS SERVICING BAY—BENEATH WHICH CAN BE SEEN EXTERNAL SHEILD PLATES OF NANO-MINIATURIZED NUCLEAR BATTERY (REQUIRES CHANGING ABOUT ONCE EVERY 30 YEARS)

'HIP' PIVOT

'KNEE' PIVOT

'ANKLE' PIVOT

LAB GROWN QUASI-HUMAN CORTEXION SIMULATING CERTAIN AREAS OF THE HUMAN BRAIN BUT OF HONEYCOMB STRUCTURE

'6TH SENSE' QUASI-PSIONIC ESPER 'EYE'

KOBALLIUM-C CHIP MODULES (FOR LOGIC AND MEMORY FUNCTIONS)

PAIRED NEUROPTIC LENSES PERFORMING SIMILAR FUNCTION TO HUMAN EYES BUT WITH ZOOM, WIDE-ANGLE, X-RAY AND INFRA RED FACILITIES (ALSO HYNOP-SUBDUE FACILITY FOR USE AGAINST TRUCULENT HUMANS)

QUASI-NERVE EXTERNAL ACCESS WIRES

VOICE-SIMULATION TANNO-CHAMBERS

BIOT 'QUASI-SENSITIVE' DIGITS

BODY CORE—VIRTUALLY A MULTI-FUNCTION BUILD-UP OF NANO-MINIATURIZED FLUIDIC CHIPS OF INCOMPREHENSIBLE COMPLEXITY

HOLOGRAPHIC WARNING PRO-JECTOR (WITH AUTO-LINK TO CENTRAL COMPUTER COMPLEXES—THUS ABLE TO DRAW ON THE VISUAL PRESEN-TATION OF OVER 20,000 LANGUAGES)

TORSO ATTACK DEFLECTION PLATES

LUBRICATION MAIN DISTRI-BUTION TUBE (LUBRICANT USUALLY NUON-PLUS FROM THE HEAD CAVITY OF SPECIALLY BRED RIGELLIAN CACHALOTS)

MULTI-PURPOSE THERMAL DRIVER AND ION DIFFRACTION DRILL (FOR ON-THE-SPOT REPAIR JOBS WHERE ATTEMPTED SECURITY PENE-TRATIONS HAVE BEEN MADE)—IN HOLSTER

INTERNAL 'LEG' STRUCTURE (SEE ARM DETAILS)

MAIN NUCLEAR-BATTERY HOUSING BENEATH ACCESS SHROUD CAN BE SEEN PLASMA/ION MONITORING COILS FOR MATTER/ANTI-MATTER CONTROLLED RELEASE CHAMBERS. NUCLEAR BATTERY HAS LIFE OF ABOUT 30 YEARS BEFORE REQUIRED CHANGE. THE 'POWER' PROFILE AND GENERAL PERFORMANCE (PHYSICAL) OF THE BIOT IS GOVERNED BY THIS BATTERY

CAPTION: *RIGHT*

TITLE: *CYBORG*

The Cyborg was first developed in the early 21st century on the planet Earth and then used particularly in international guerilla warfare. The example on this page is of one of the earlier primitive models, the Cyborg Attack 1, here running at around fifty kilometres per hour in a limited localised attack on a United Western power camp in the Andes Territory. It carried a positronic brain system and various in-built weaponry and was a devastating adversary on the personal battlefield. For further details see page 38, robot list.

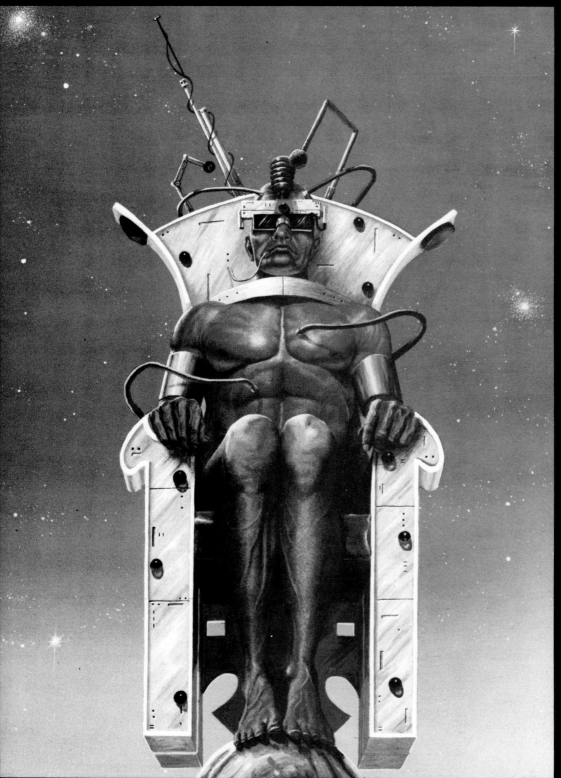

CAPTION: *LEFT*

TITLE: *SETcon*

The picture on this page is an artist's impression of the first stages of the SETcon; the operation used on Charybdis for converting humans with the planet's devasting endemic cancer into Mandroids; 90% bionic and 10% human. The early parts of the operations seal in the brain tissue and reinforce the skull with various hardening materials, mainly bio-plastic. At the same time tests are carried out as to the resistance of the individual's tissue to his advancing cancer via the tubes attached to the patient's chest and stomach. For further details see glossary, pages 114/7 and for female counterpart see page 37.

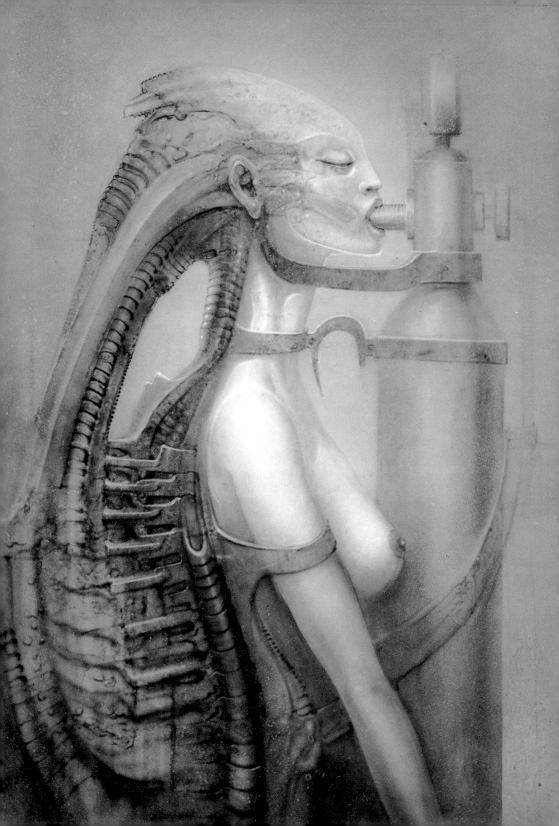

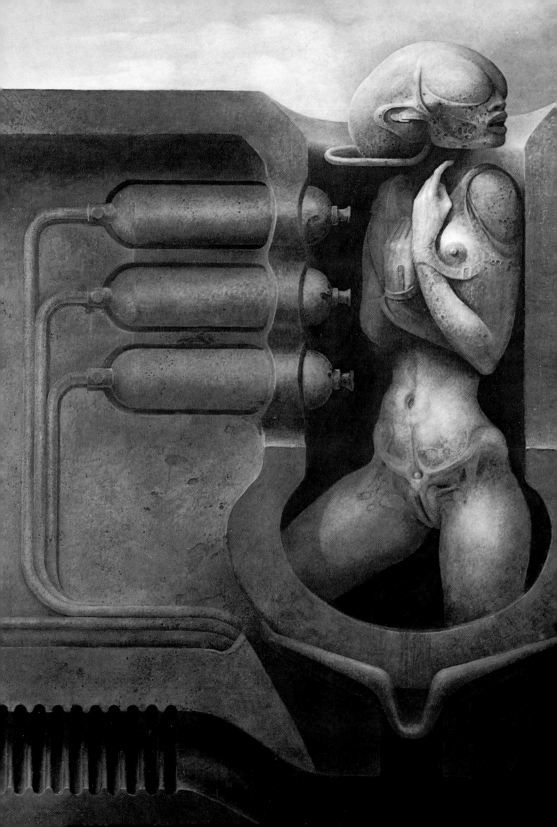

# WEAPONS AND SPACE GEAR

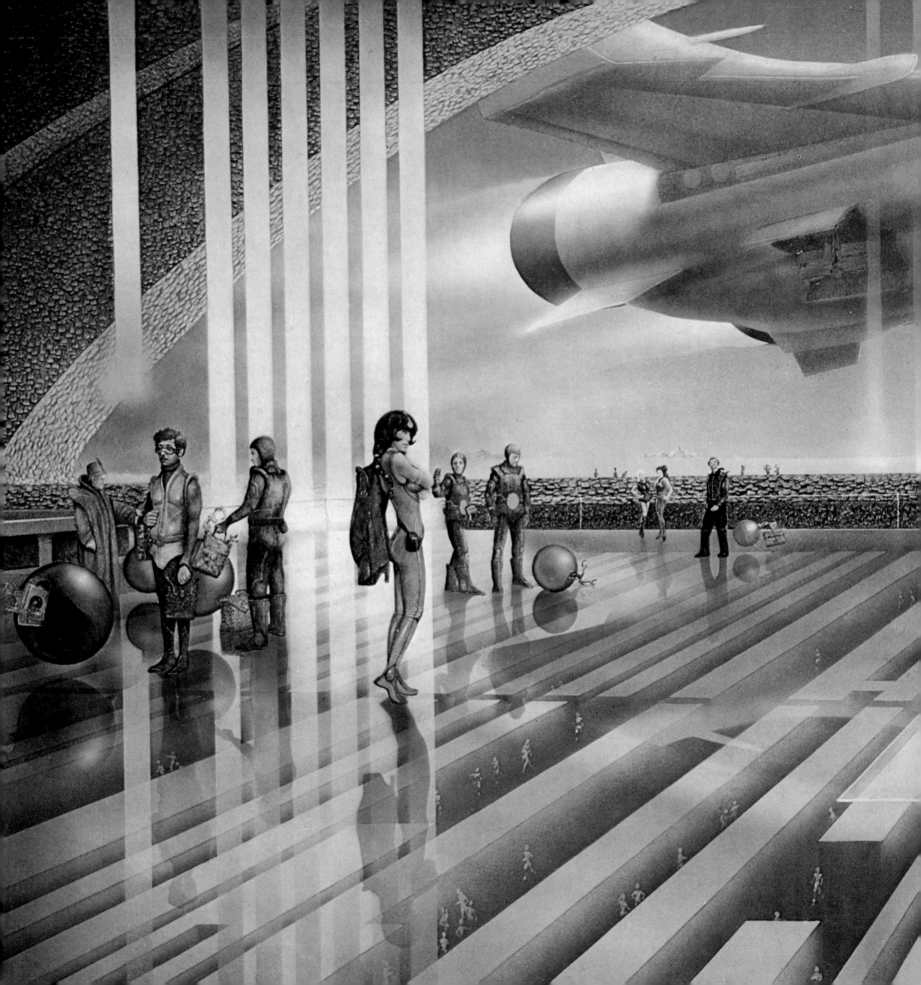

# MECHANISMO-FILE PRINTOUT

TITLE: SOL TRANSIT COMPLEX 7 (JANUS)

E-DATE:

INDEX RETRIEVAL KEY:

SECURITY STANCE:    ACCESS:    SHEET NUMBER: 2    TOTAL: 2    SHEETS

DUPLICATION:    COPIES    THIS COPY NUMBER:    ASSIGNED TO:    MICRO-FILE RECALL CODE:

Talian and offer his services in some mercenary capacity. Dazhbog succeeded in creating havoc, after Talian accepted his offer, amongst the Sirius System, making hit and run attacks on all manner of Axis targets. He thus earned large sums of money from the Shards and traded with Axis under a disguise, taking their money and then blowing them out of the Universe wherever his luck would allow. Eventually it ran out, however, and he was identified while on a bogus commercial attaché trip to Novo Russe War Ministry. While making a dash across a Neorganika-defined auto-highway he slipped and was sucked into the vacuum-grab of a robo detritus-conversion unit where he was rendered, along with the detritus, into plant fertilizer. There is a small plot of land in the middle of a field on Sirius IV where the cabbages are said to grow 12 feet across!

In the centre-ground of the picture is a famed member of the 'Oldest Profession', dressed in the green clothing of Legal Space Courtesan, Diamond Class. Two more, lowly classed women can be seen in the background, the one in black being of the class of 'Space Whore'. The girl in green is THELXEPEIA VRIKSHAKA DE 10 and her availability ruby glows 'On'. She waits to catch Dazhbog's eye and he will enjoy an expensive but innovative night on her Null-grav oil-bed.

The little fellow wearing the life-enhancing lenses (worn generally by people of depressive dispositions and tailored to individual comp-profile and psyche lesion zone record), is a company accountant with the trans-stellar giant Earth General Positronics and Sub-Particle Exotica Inc., a job designed to render anyone depressive. ERIC SMALLPIECE, for that is the accountant's name, felt he was the only person who realised that General Positronics' production capacity fell far short of the total required for the accumulated business and that the horrendous wartime penalty clauses the company would eventually find itself saddled with, would topple it overnight. He was later proven to be correct. Poor Eric believed that he was to blame and has in this illustration decided to offer his services as a proxy-leper on Bootes XX. Inadvertently, however, he managed to board the wrong craft and ended up on Janus, muttering "I have to become a proxy-leper". The man to hear his words was MAGNIFICO EL DORADO, the Thrice Enlightened, self-appointed head and sole member of the Church of the 'Thrice Hourly Ablutions', to be seen in the extreme left of the picture. Eric became the first new member of the cult, to be known as 'Eric the Splendid'.

The small round devices scattered about the station are PORTAMECKS. These robotic devices, used for transporting baggage were some 120 years old when the illustration was completed and one appears to have given up the ghost at last, presently being surveyed by ground staff.

At the rear centre-right of the picture, being followed by a suitcase carrying Portameck is BYRON Q MIDGARD, the man with the most amazing tale in the whole gathering.

Born in 2595 SGT on the planet Achamandura, he volunteered in 2625 to make a time insertion into the past, in the hideously dangerous Paterson TD 39 time dilation vehicle. His trip ended up as one of the 84 time travel accidents prior to the building of the TD 45 'Tempus Frangit', and his person, intact in both mind and body, appears at irregular points in time and space for periods varying from a microsecond to many years. He appears not to age at all as a result of this phenomenon (which we call the Paterson Chronofractus-Disfuncto Miserere) but despite his effective but curiously impermanent immortality, his peculiar advantages can hardly appeal to us. In his book 'The Greatest Joke of All', the manuscript of which was found lying on an atom-tram seat on the planet Pustulus VII he outlines some of the many lives, long and short, pleasant and unpleasant, he has lived, through millions of years of space-time history.

(For further details of Midgard's story see newspaper report—pp.116/117).

STATIONERY RE-ORDER MATRIX KEY (I B M. ONLY) 02 002 0001 — AN ORDER TODAY SAVES DELAY!    MESSRS. CROYDON & KRYPTON LTD. — MANUFACTURERS OF ''A-STANDARD'' DATA CONTROL SYSTEMS SINCE 1987 — BY APPOINTMENT.

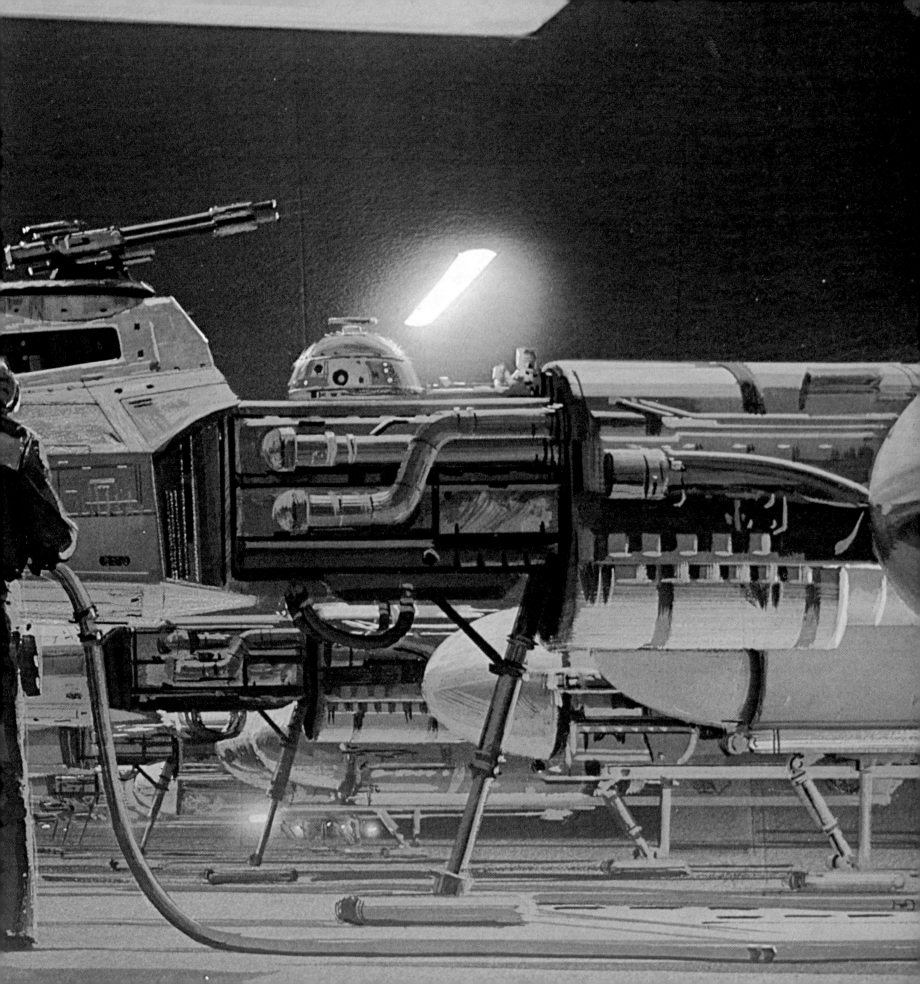

CAPTION:

52|53

TITLE:

STAR WARS SPACE
STATION

Star Wars space station.
McQuarry produced the
original illustrations that
formed the basis for most of
the major scenes in the
movie Star Wars. The
scene on the previous two
pages took place toward the
end of the story when
preparations were being
made to attack Death Star.

WHAT DOES THE WELL DRESSED SPACEMAN—or woman wear to work? The reality as we know it today is pretty uninteresting. American astronauts are stuffed into bulbous space garb than makes them look like shaved teddy bears topped with golden domes. The Soviets, who send their cosmonauts aloft in a shirtsleeve environment, really have missed the boat completely. Instead of snazzy space outfits, *Star Trek* or *Space 1999* would have been happy to supply designs, they dress their solid Slavs in proletarian boiler suits. Not good at all. Couldn't they have taken a peek at the old SF magazines to find some more interesting ideas? This sort of research has noble antecedents so there is nothing to be ashamed of. During the Second World War two SF writer-engineers worked on the development of high altitude flying suits: Robert Heinlein and L. Sprague deCamp. They took as the models for their first designs artwork from the science fiction magazines. Illustrations for stories they had written themselves.

Of course they used the most up-to-date and practical designs, for in the beginning the spacesuits were unusual to say the least. The design was always massive, some of them appeared to have been made of riveted battleship armour, since the artists did not realise that only about five pounds to the square inch pressure would have to be contained. The occupants of these monstrosities had to peer out through tiny windows and, with little chance of walking, were propelled by tractor treads on the soles of their boots. Nor were the artists quite clear as to what tools might be needed, so the poor spacemen are lumbered with such practical items as coils of rope, hatchets, spades (for digging lunar latrines?) and even the occasional boat-hook. Equally impractical were the supplies of oxygen, usually contained in a tank about the size of a beer can fixed to the back of the helmet.

This unhappy state of affairs continued for years, right up to the advent of the space opera pulps, notably the immortal *Planet Stories*. On their covers, as well as in the interior illustrations, we can trace the development and ready acceptance of sexual dimorphism in space. While still earthbound, mankind is not noted for radical physical differences between the sexes. Of course there *are* differences, but none of them as obvious as say the elephant seal where he is five times bigger than she and looks like a totally different species. Yet once mankind and womankind head for the stars radical differences begin to appear. The men, being keenly aware of the rigours of space, wear one-piece suits made from some thick and barely flexible substance. Their boots are more cumbersome than those of a Russian peasant, while clumsy gloves protect their hands. A transparent fishbowl affair covers their heads, complete with traditional tiny air tank. There is a consistent logic to this which we can appreciate when we consider the cold airlessness of space.

But what about the girls? They are indeed badly treated and very much in need of an intergalactic femlib movement. They are clad in bikinis, or skin-tight bathing suits, instead of the woollen undies the men are sure to be wearing. We know this because the ladies' spacesuits are made of cellophane or some other flexible and transparent substance. Their light gloves would be better off worn to the opera, and they sport the interesting novelty of high-heeled space boots. The glass helm is the only item of gear they share with the males.

There is a mystery here because the reason for the difference in space garb is never explained in the stories themselves. In fact the cover usually stands on its own and illustrates no story in the magazine. Why are the girls dressed so differently from the men? Even when they get out of space gear the future appears to hold unusual clothing patterns for them. The heroes explore jungle and desert planets in sensible engineers' boots and puttees—but not the heroines. They sport bare legs and bared midriffs and usually shield their interesting upper regions with brass breastplates. These metal brassieres appear to have been turned out by an insane lingerie machinist. Surely they would be hideously uncomfortable; damp and dripping in summer, chill in the winter. What is going on here?

Pretty obviously the artwork has more to do with sex than science. There can surely be no physical reason for different garb for the sexes when in the same environment. So if it is sex—who is it that would like to look at girls with very little clothes on? Why boys of course, and grown-up boys, even young men—the readers of the pulps where these exotic illustrations appeared. Perhaps these readers were too young or too shy to touch girls—but you can always look. And what they were looking at, all that long and lovely hair, boots and gloves, hints of fetishism, while it has more than a soupçon of sadism to it with the often present whips and chains. And that means sex, yes it does, good old sex for that is what fetishism and sadism are all about. There was plenty of this kind of thing around in the cleaner-than-clean pulps; if not in the stories surely in the art. Nor was this completely by accident; girls on covers sell magazines. The stories delivered daydreams, escape and excitement. The art put a bit of sex into the dreams and no one minded at all.

As spaceship design has improved down through the years, so have living standards aboard ship. This development has continued in films and television until our spaceships have grown as big as battleships. It is shirt-sleeve environment all the way now, and both sexes wear basically the same uniforms while on duty. Rank differences aboard ship are on the way out, resembling the Air Force more than the Navy. Only when spacefarers venture from the air-conditioned comfort of their vessels does the need for protective garbing become urgent.

Spacesuit design has improved too, with the steady march of technology being greatly appreciated by the SF writers. Fast reading, digital and projected instrument readouts, are being perfected both for high speed fighters and space vehicles today. Some of this information is already displayed inside the pilot's helmet; eventually it will all be done that way inside a spacesuit helmet. SF technology advances far faster than the real one so that many spacesuits have become really small space lifeboats that not only protect the occupant from the harsh realities of space, but feed and drain him, provide radio and other communication, navigational aids, and even a drive of some sort to bring him to safety. The physical size of these new spacesuits is never described, but surely microminiaturisation can only go so far. Food, water, power plant, drive, fuel must all take up a bit of space. I have a feeling that this sort of spacesuit would have to be about as big as a Rolls Royce with the hardy traveller sticking out of one end.

Warfare makes great demands on technology, and the warfare of the future can only continue this trend. Nevertheless in its basic aims a future war will be no different from our contemporary version. While bombs and machines can destroy the enemy, it will still take soldiers to occupy and hold the territory so gained. So, heads high, GI Joe and Private Atkins appear to be marching into the future. However, since they will be doing their job in space and in the hostile environment of alien worlds, they must be protected by some variation of the spacesuit. And there is more to making a spacesuit militarily acceptable than welding on a sergeant's stripes. The first thing to do is of course to armour it—and we are right back to the first riveted tanks that graced the pulp magazines covers. Once protected they have to be armed as well, and powered and fuelled. So what we end up with is a one-man fighting machine as described in Heinlein's *Starship Trooper* or Haldeman's *The Forever War*■

# MECHANISMO PLAN PRINTOUT

MACHINE: **LIGHT SABRE**

MODEL NUMBER/TYPE: **ACME STANDARD**
E-DATE: **3535·03·31**
INDEX RETRIEVAL KEY: **□△○772⊠**
SECURITY STANCE: **SECURITY "A"**
ACCESS: **JEDI KNIGHTS**
MICRO-FILE RECALL CODE: **01·373·3404**

1. Nucleonic pill embedded in resinated organic shield [menseric dielectric core].
2. Exogerized fibronic container for [1].
3. Degaussing lenses.
4. Affiliated transfonic lenses. Multi-directional.
5. Neonic control switch [for controlling polarity of [1] to enable lenses to generate light waves to specified length and intensity].
6. Lobomotic energizer.
7. Directional coil-lateral.
8. Directional coil—sub-horizontal.
9. Laser generator crystal-rubionic nodules.
10. Self energising control coil.
11. Inhibitor negativised hexonic plates.
12. Nozzle.
13. Colt housing.
14. Laser housing — organically shielded.
15. Lens housing.
16. Therminoic generator housing —formic shielded.
17. Chromonic handle.
18. Mounting ring . . . Swivel located.

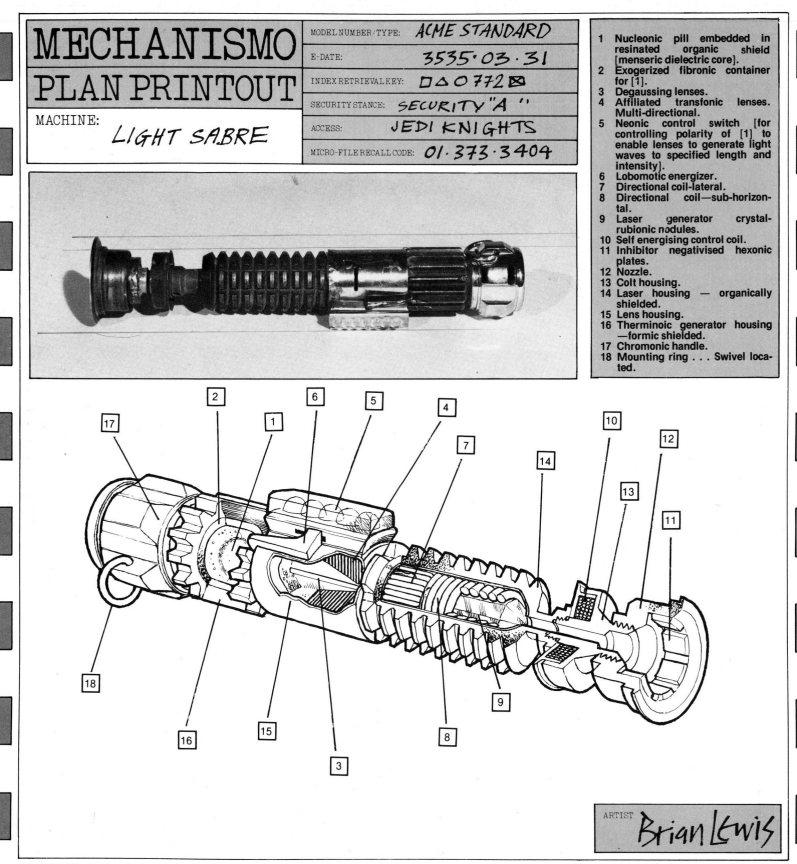

ARTIST **Brian Lewis**

# MECHANISMO
# PLAN PRINTOUT

MACHINE:

*STARWARS BLASTER*

MODEL NUMBER/TYPE: *3D GEN*

E-DATE: *3537 · 01 · 14*

INDEX RETRIEVAL KEY: *0△□314⊠*

SECURITY STANCE: *SECURITY 'B MINUS'*

ACCESS: *U.C.M.W. STUDENTS.*

MICRO-FILE RECALL CODE: *01 · 274 · 8842*

1 Ultrasonic self seeking all purpose sight
2 Infra red lens
3 Fibre vision rods
4 Electron gun
5 Electron optidirectional vision mixer
6 Ultra sonic parameter separator
7 Ultrasonic feedback parallex chamber
8 Generator connection
9 Ultrasonic generator crystal
10 Ion-laser mixer
11 Ion mixer generator
12 Ultrasonic vision store
13 Back-up for 12
14 Sight adjuster
15 Ionised vacuum and housing
16 Laser crystal
17 Laser generator gun—self-repeating
18 Impaction coil assembly
19 Ion battery — Chromon contact inserts
20 Gas restrictor safety catch
21 Reaction particles
22 Diaphragm
23 Gas control valve
24 Gas way
25 Gas valve to insulation control
26 Handle mounting catch
27 Trigger and guard
28 Single shot / repeat switch
29 Butt
30 Ion condenser / accelerator
31 Outer barrel
32 Inner vacuumised codeine insulated barrel
33 Nozzle adjuster
34 Adjustable spray or stream nozzle
35 Foresight
36 Stand
37 Stand catch
38 Pre-set ion mixer control

ARTIST: *Brian Lewis*

CAPTION:
THIS SPREAD

TITLE:
THE CABAL

The Cabal. Chris Achilleos is the artist for this scene depicting a battle in space, on the Bridges of Grief, in a novel entitled The Cabal by Saul Dunn.

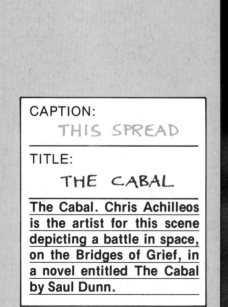

CAPTION:

PAGES 64/65

TITLE:

ACHAMANDURA

The planet of Achamandura in the system of Pass 4 within the outlying territories of the Capellan Shards is the only known planet where five 'Walking cities' were actually constructed and inhabited for nearly 200 years. The cities were called 'Cybertectural Animots' by their inventor and designer, Pan Hinderis, and although Hinderis did not live to see his architectural vision realised he is credited with the first complete and effective blueprints. His 'walking cities' were 2.3 kilometres tall and capable of housing and servicing 400,000 people in space and comfort. They were built experimentally as an attempt to colonise the rock-hard Wastes of Achamandura; the cities were largely self-sufficient, recycling waste, water and power. They used massive magnetic forces to provide stability and effect the 'walking' — a slow but steady perambulation at around 5 kilometres per Achamanduran day (about 4 Earth days). This was Pan's bizarre touch; his professional life was dedicated to providing environ-

*Continued next page*

NTELLIGENCE allowed mankind to build tools. These tools aided the escape from a hand-to-mouth existence of the hunting-gathering culture, which in turn led to the existence of the city state. With the cities came leisure—for a few—and with leisure there was time for thinking, time to develop the arts and sciences. So the existence of the city is inextricably linked with the foundation of science and the continuing existence of science. Science fiction has paid its due to its demi-namesake by presenting bigger, better and more exciting cities than any ever seen on the face of the Earth. Only recently have the writers begun to see cities as places of oppression for mankind; after all there have been more rural hells than urban ones in our history. Memory is fleeting so we should keep reminding ourselves that right up to the end of the nineteenth century, and well into the twentieth, all the real action; intellectual, artistic, social financial—took place in the cities. The creative people left their bucolic backgrounds and made their way to London or New York or the major city of their choice. Emily Dickinson wrote that she never saw a train, going anywhere, that she did not want to board. This is meaningless to a happily ensconced city dweller, but elicits a depth of response from someone of intellectual ambitions buried in Booniesville.

So writers who loved cities designed bigger and better ones for the future. Wells in *The Sleeper Awakes* had the sleeper wake up in a city full of gadgets and transportation and communication wonders. Almost all the book length utopias have been citified utopias. Then, when the pulps began churning along, cities grew in complexity and design. Just as with the spaceship a universal super-city came into existence, a concept shared in common by writers and illustrators. Stories could be set in this city without going into too much background or detail. The reader accepted eagerly and read on.

The city was big and unified, well designed and usually wholly automatic. All of the service industries, power, water, food and such were down in the basement, a super sub-city of "ways" and tunnels and great hulking machines. Anything bad that happened in the city usually happened down here. Above were the spearing towers, the spanning bridges, the open gardens and moving ways. Offices, shops, theatres, dwellings, rising up higher and higher to the landing pads right up there on the top. (Unlike the helicopter on the Pan Am Building in New York, these flying vehicles never fell off and dropped on the citizenry below.) These futuristic cities were so well designed that they could literally run themselves. Giving rise to numerous plots where the cities keep on going after the original inhabitants had left.

But city growth has it limits, reached in Asimov's Foundation series with the planet-wide city of Trantor. (Transformed to Helior and examined in some depth in Harrison's *Bill, the Galactic Hero*.) There is a natural limit to this kind of growth; once you have the super city built you can either keep it running or destroy it. Or move it to a new dimension.

Under water. Up until Verne's *20,000 Leagues Under the Sea* very little attention was paid to matters below the ocean's surface. He changed all that. Not only did he invent a big and comfortable submarine, complete with fish dinners and pipe organ, but he established once and for all the glamour of life in the depths. Captain Nemo invented scuba gear, and used electricity to drive, light and heat his sub, to manufacture oxygen and even to charge up his electric bullets. The next step after living in the sub was living in an underwater city and the pulps ran them up by the hundred. O'Donnell's *Fury* in 1950 had a giant pressure dome over the entire city, but separate, connected domes were a popular theme as well.

After the cities on Earth there of course came cities in space. The history of these constructs is more ancient than usually believed for the first city in space, a satellite of the Earth, was launched into position in 1869 by Edward Everett Hale in his story ''The Brick Moon''. His moon is made of brick—what a salvation to the building trades this must have been!—and is 200 feet in diameter. When completed it is due to be hurled into space by giant flywheels to place it in orbit and used as an aid to celestial navigation. (An early forerunner of the navigation satellites in use today.) However, as in many an SF story, something goes wrong, and it is accidentally flipped up into space a little too early and all of the bricklayers and their families, who are living aboard while the thing is being built, go along with it. At a height of 9,000 miles it goes into orbit where its inhabitants find life quite enjoyable.

Satellite design has been improved since there—it could hardly have gotten worse—and space around a thousand planets has been filled with populated satellites of all kinds. Factories, power generating satellites, spaceship stations, war satellites. All of them have to be built in space, with the exception of James Blish's Cities in Flight series. Great antigravity machines called spindizzies are put into position around Manhattan Island—and lift the entire heart of New York City into space. A dazzling concept indeed. New York followed by other cities who leave the tired economies of Earth for the excitement of the stars.

Then, for many years, the biggest city in space was in Clifford Simak's ''Limiting Factor'' where the spacemen discover an artificial metal world that is so big that, when they explore it, they can make no sense of it at all. Although this world, and all the others, are small time when compared with the concept of the physicist Frederick Dyson. He speculated that if all of the planets of the solar system were ground up and melted down, there would be enough material available to form a thin sphere about the sun, a giant shell that could be inhabited on its inner surface. There would be no Shaw in *Orbitsville*, which though written earlier was not published until

*From previous page*

mental stimulation for the jaded senses of city dwellers. No more such cities were built after the five reached the end of their life span.

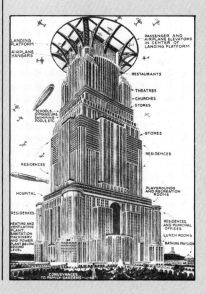

1. Solar energy is available full time at a rate of 1.4 kilowatts/m² almost ten times higher than at Earth's surface, averaged over one year, and never cut off by night.

2. The cylinders are closed with hemispherical endcaps containing oxygen. The cylinders rotate providing on the inner surface an Earth-normal gravity.

3. The cylinder circumference divides into six regions, three valleys alternating with three arrays of windows.

4. Light planar mirrors.

5. Small crop growing cylinders.

6. Blue tinted solars to give impression of blue sky.

7. Large plane-surfaced mirrors attached by cables for sunlight reflection.

*General points:* (a) *The Island Three Space Colony would be twenty miles long and four miles in diameter. The living areas, agricultural and industrial area would be located within a few miles of one another but would have separately chosen temperature, climate, day-length and gravity controls.* (b) *The mountains formed inside the cylinders for living areas could have a height of up to 10,000 feet.* (c) *The mirrors reflecting the sunlight can be controlled so that the angle of sunlight varies. As the mirrors open in the morning so the sun will rise.*

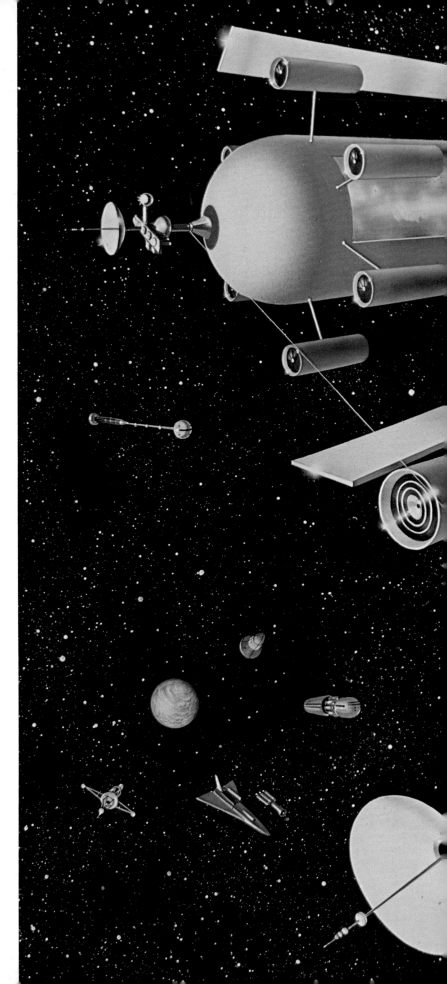

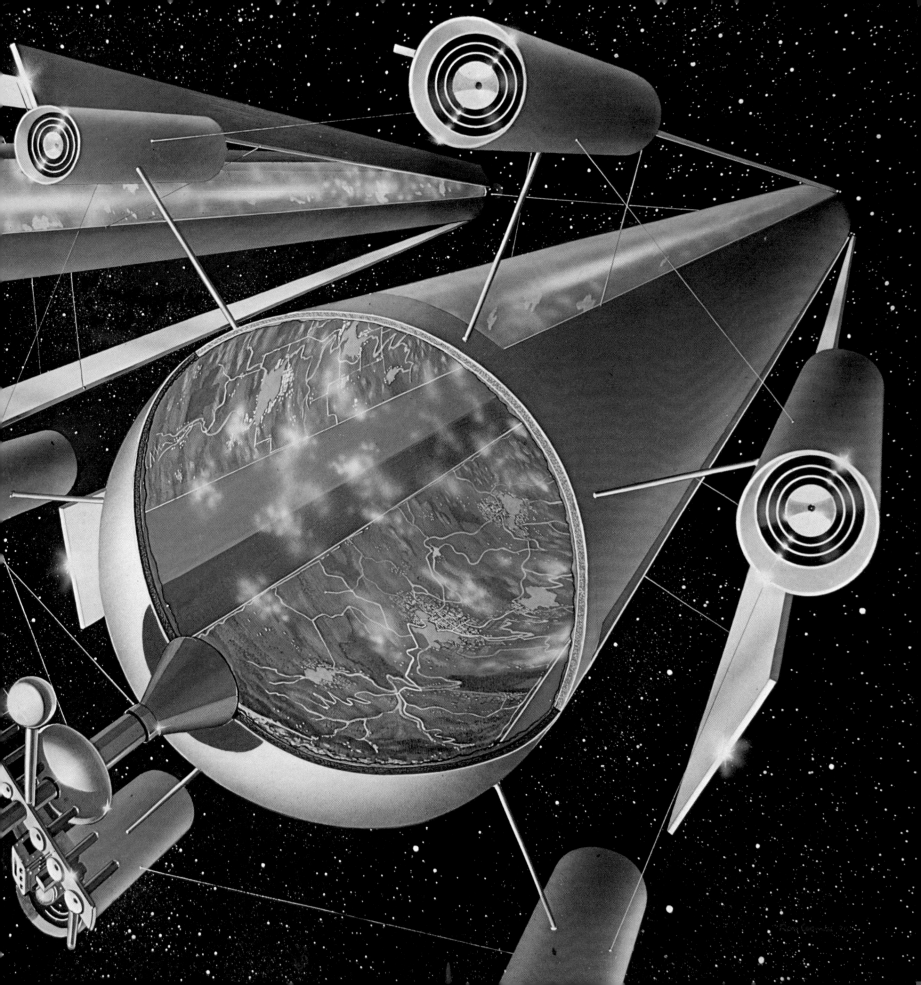

CAPTION:

## PAGE 71

TITLE:

## DAZHBOG

**Dazhbog entering Siricity II, the old capital of the Sirius Axis Empire. A master of disguise, Dazhbog, here on a counter-intelligence brief for vice-Marshall Talian, sports the quaint uniform of the Sirius Civil Service. The 1000-year old city, no longer the nerve-centre of the Empire's military operations, has relaxed into becoming one of the main tourist attractions and housing the Civil Service admin complex. For Dazhbog's usual appearance see page 49; biog. page 50/1.**

sun to permit an endless balmy summer. This design was first used by Bob Shaw in *Orbitsville*, which though written earlier was not published until 1975. Here the Earth explorers zip into the sphere and must spend years getting back to the entrance they originally came in through. This Dyson design was also used later by Larry Niven in *Ringworld* (1970), though he limited himself to a single band in space rather than a sphere.

The alien inhabitants of other planets, circling distant suns, are pretty dab hands at city building too. In E.E. Smith's Lensman series, as well as his earlier galaxy-exploring novels—we have a look-in at some of these. But for every inhabited alien city we find in SF there must be a dozen ruined ones. Exploring them is fun—as well as being dangerous—and rarely so well done as by Beam Piper in "Omnilingual" where our scientists learn to translate the records of a vanished alien race. Sounds impossible—until the author explains logically just how it can be accomplished.

On a much larger scale is Arthur C. Clarke's wandering planet in *Rendezvous with Rama*, where an entire world-city comes whistling through our solar system.

But inner-city violence seems to have put paid to the day of the really super super city. Authors are now returning to nature, the village and the isolated house in the hills. The great cities are either dismembered or allowed to fall into ruins, warnings to the youth of the future of the error of their ancestors' ways■

Details of 'Island Three Space Colony' (artist's impressions). The ground on which houses are built need only be two feet thick. Windows set at an angle in one wall could show the immensity of space and the brilliant unclouded stars would also be visible, drifting across the field of view in the two-minute rotational cycle.

Each individual cylinder can have its own access to space for taking on products and for waste disposal. Workers would travel to and from work in a large air-filled zero-gravity corridor, pushing off from their starting points and drifting in free flight to their destinations.

Given the two rotational cylinders in space, parallel to each other and only fifty miles apart, the space dwellers will be able to take advantage of the rotation which produces Earth-normal gravity in the habitat valleys. For Island Three, that rotation is at a rate of about four hundred miles per hour. A simple vehicle, less complicated than a terrestrial bus could contain spacious seating and require no engine or crew. As its passengers board it, walking down stairs through their island valley as if they were entering a subway station, the vehicle will still be locked to the outer surface of the habitat. When the door is closed and sealed, a computer on the habitat will wait until the correct moment in the next two-minute rotation cycle, then will unlock the vehicle. Proceeding through space on a straight line, with the four hundred miles per hour tangential velocity of the habitat the vehicle will arrive at the other cylinder in less than eight minutes.

Pedal craft will be used to travel in the low gravity areas at the centre of the habitat cylinders where gravity will be some 3 per cent of Earth-normal. This will be at an elevation of some 7000 feet above the valley floor where a 'flyer' will weigh only 30 per cent as much as he would on Earth.

# FANTASTIC

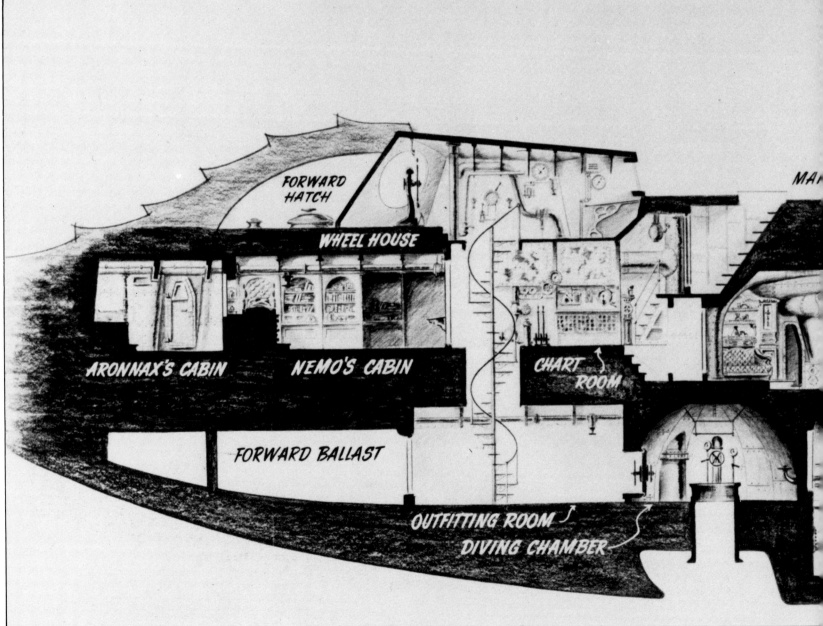

FORWARD HATCH

WHEEL HOUSE

MA...

ARONNAX'S CABIN

NEMO'S CABIN

CHART ROOM

FORWARD BALLAST

OUTFITTING ROOM
DIVING CHAMBER

# MACHINES

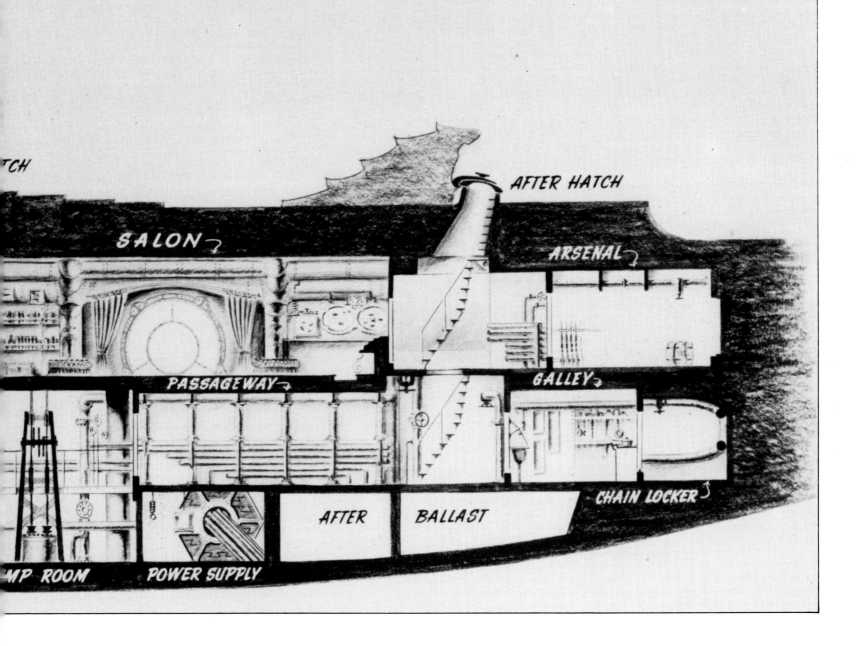

CAPTION:

THIS SPREAD

TITLE:

BIG PLANET

Big Planet — a novel by Jack Vance. The illustration is by Jim Burns and depicts a form of transport used by the populace living on one of the largest inhabited planets in fiction.

# FLYING MACHINES

T HE MACHINES in science fiction are vital to its existence — surely SF is the only form of fiction that dares to have a hunk of hardware as hero. A quick look at antique SF art reveals that the earliest piece of hardware was the flying machine. It is pretty obvious that Leonardo's helicopter would never have gotten off the ground, no matter how hard the man flapped, but it is surely a more practical design than the pinwheels-on-masts that were supposed to propel Jules Verne's *The Clipper of the Clouds* (1886). Undoubtedly the most unrealistic, yet most utterly charming, flying machines were those of the illustrator Harry Grant Dart. His preposterous planes have wings and propellers, and there is only the occasional glimpse of a dirigible. For a long time these were thought to be the aerial transportation of the future, as in Kipling's "With the Night Mail". This theme was amplified to exhaustion by H.G. Wells in 1907 in *The War in the Air*, where a fleet of these giant craft first bomb the United States, then launch an airborne invasion. The plot moves briskly along after that with Great Britain and France attacking Germany, being topped only by the Asians joining the fight with airships of their own. The crash of the *Von Hindenburg* and the *S-100*, along with the accelerating growth of aeronautic science, put paid to the dirigible menace.

Earliest credit for the more exotic forms of aerial transportation must be given to Phil Nowlan and Dick Calkins, the creators of *Buck Rogers*. Generations of preconceptions were shaped by this seminal comic strip. Professor Jamieson's anti-grav chute in A.E. Van Vogt's ''Co-operate or Else'' is nothing more than Buck's film-can, backpack, jumping belt writ large. Nor does it take an exceptionally keen eye to see the resemblance between his rocket belt and James Bond's modern equivalent. Equally seminal were the force field legs that supported the warships of the evil Red Mongols. Those legs are still stamping through the pages of SF.

In the 1930's, while real aeroplanes were still being made of bamboo and bailing wire, the winged intellects of the SF writers were flying faster and further into the future. Unhampered by any aeronautical knowledge, Stanley Weinbaum's intercontinental jets blasted between continents in ''The Wheels of If'', while the technocratic saviours in *Things to Come* flew in from Basra in gorgeously impractical flying palaces.

The master of the flying machine—as he was master of all SF machinery —was of course Frank R. Paul. This patient teutonic artist slave of the Luxembourg publishing fiend, Hugo Gernsback, gave graphic existence to the SF ideas of the thirties. Not only did Paul's aircraft burst from the pages of *Amazing*, they whizzed their way towards the covers of *Science and Mechanics*.

This brief period of aerial enthusiasm was interrupted by World War II when there was a geometric progression in plane design. (The wingspan of the B-29 bomber was greater than the total distance first flown by the Wright brothers a few decades earlier.) With reality overtaking their imaginations, SF writers abandoned the competition and jumped directly into antigravity. The recent success of hovercraft, surface effect vessels that support themselves on a cushion of air, have brought these vehicles into SF, but this is obvious parasitism from reality since the SF authors didn't have the brains to invent the things themselves.

(The ''floaters'' that have floated through many a story have no connection with these later vehicles; they were powered by radium or magic or other unexplained source of lifting energy.)

The ultimate in aerial transportation must be psi force where the person involved just wills himself to a new location, leaving and arriving apparently instantaneously. This does help to speed up the plot, and can produce masterpieces such as A. Bester's *Stars My Destination* where an entire civilisation ''jaunts'' in this manner□

CAPTION:

THIS SPREAD

TITLE:

GRAY PRINCE

**Gray Prince — a novel by Jack Vance. The illustration is by Jim Burns and depicts the hero of the story whose skin is artificially tinted blue and who always wears grey. He stands beside a land yacht, capable of massive speed.**

# MACHINES

ANY FORM OF FICTION where an idea or a machine can be the hero of a story *must* be concerned with the very nature of the machinery involved. The great strength of SF is this constant examination and re-examination of the state of the craft. There is never any need for technological obsolescence in SF as there is in the real external world—as for example on the London docks where up until very recently a steam powered crane built in the last century was still in daily use. Not so in SF! Great computers are built in an instant—to be replaced by even greater and better computers as soon as new theories are proposed.

This is particularly true in the SF war story where applied technology is the going thing. As early as 1884 Robert Grant introduced electrically charged bullets in his novel *The King's Men*. The production lines of wartime hardware really started clanking in 1898 when Wells' Martians in *The War of the Worlds* landed in spaceships and marched forth in tripedal war machines. Wells, though believing in peace, went out of his way to show the horrors of technological warfare. In ''The Land Ironclads'' he invented the armoured tank, then in *The World Set Free* he described atomic bombs being dropped from planes—although he did have them being thrown overboard by hand. By 1933 he was in full swing and in *The Shape of Future Things to Come* he wrote about supertanks, aerial bombardment, gas warfare and all of the rest of the war machines that have been rattling through science fiction ever since.

Edgar Rice Burroughs took the battles off the Earth into space in 1914 with *A Princess of Wars*. The Martians, both red and green, travelled in bathtub shaped aircraft propelled by rays, firing radium bullets from radar-equipped guns. Warfare is warming up, and things really improved with the publication of *Amazing* in 1926. Soon there were stories like Stanton Coblentz's "After 12,000 years" where warplanes of the future drop giant poisonous insects onto each other's territory. In *The Green Man of Graypec* (1935) Festus Pragnell invented desert tank warfare, while in *The World Below* (1924) S. Fowler Wright depicts a world-wide war in the far future where the flying craft are giant artificial insects, the weapons sheets of energy.

It was those masters of the big-screen, star-smashing story, E.E. Smith and John W. Campbell, who really got war into space and moving on a singularly imposing scale. Not just spaceships but entire fleets—and fleets of fleets—blasted off, and were often blasted out of existence. The armoured spacesuit grew stronger and stronger, spaceaxes clanked, blasters roared, screen after screen of defensive force fields went down under the irresistible attack of ravening rays, and the universe has never been the same since. Presser beams fought against tractor beams, space torpedoes were knocked out by disintegrator rays, while race after race of evil aliens were blown into their component atoms. The galactic war—impossible though it may seem—continues to be a stock in trade of the SF writer, and the galactic empire as well.

Individual weaponry has long been an industry in itself. Hand blasters, rocket guns, recoilless pistols, defensive force fields have been trotted out in legions, enough to blast the mind if not the enemy. And things are still hotting up on the screen and the box. Phasers and lasers flash through *Star Trek*, while *Star Wars* has enlarged the armoury with light sabres and a vast selection of hand-held energy weapons, not to mention spatial dogfights and a planet-destroying artificial world.

On the more constructive side SF has produced some fascinating forms of transportation. As early as 1849 in "Mellonta Tauta" Edgar Allan Poe's transcontinental railroad trains were big enough to contain ballrooms for dancing the trip away. This was made possible by a fairly illogical width of 50 feet between the tracks. Wells got into the railroad act in *A Modern Utopia* with billiard rooms (untroubled by vibration?), bathrooms and libraries, in addition to the normal train fittings. Monorails had their day as well. In 1897 Francis Stockon wrote about electric trains pendant from overhead rails in *The Great Stone of Sardis*, while Wells himself in *The War in the Air* had his monorail cars zipping right across the English Channel on cables.

Away from the railroad the horse was the fastest mode of transportation, so the SF inventors dreamed about automobiles. Away back in 1880 Percy Gregg had his three wheeled cars doing a nineteenth-century ton-up in

*Across the Zodiac*. They could go "far faster than the swiftest mail coach". That is between fifteen and thirty miles an hour. Plenty of room for improvement here and by 1891, in *Freeland* Theodore Hertzka could describe with great enthusiasm his cars that were driven by great steel springs—said springs being wound up at steam-powered winding stations sited along the major roads. Wood, coal, charcoal, "therms from a little petroleum lamp", have all been utilised. And the faster they go, the better the roads they need. (Unless they are like the ur-James Bond cars in Von Hanstein's "Utopia Island" (1931) that travel on either land or sea, propelled by a combination of compressed air and magnetism.) Rocket cars made their appearance in the thirties—Buck Rogers always enjoyed driving one—giving way to automated highways, in *Methuselah's Children* by Heinlein (1941), which are still being considered as a practical traffic solution today. Specially designed vehicles, such as Arthur Clarke's moonbuggy in *A Fall of Moondust* (1961), antedate and anticipate the reality of the one that the astronauts drove.

Moving sidewalks, finally being put into use in airports today, were described fondly in Verne's *Floating Island*, as well as "moving platforms" in Stockton's *The Great Stone of Sardis*. Once again Wells led the way in *When the Sleeper Awakes* with his "moving ways". These ways are separated into lanes each moving at a greater speed, so a passenger can work across from the local to the express lane. This design was lifted bodily by Heinlein for "The Roads Must Roll" in 1940 and improved with shops, restaurants, technology, police, strikers and the rest.

Once below the ground, transportation becomes very interesting. Buck Rogers ignores certain temperature problems and has a tube going right through the planet so that cars dropped in at one end shoot out of the other. Naturally, Buck's girlfriend gets suspended in no-gravity in the centre of the Earth. Clark's world-wide tube system in "Rescue Mission" fascinates the alien saviours, while Deutsch's "A Subway Named Möbius" (1950) presents certain unexpected topological problems to riders in the train; they vanish into another dimension for a couple of weeks. Earth technology is exported into space in Colin Kapp's "The Subways of Tazoo" and its sequel, "Railways up on Canis".

The simplest form of transportation is undoubtedly MT, or matter transmission. Clarke had people broken down for transmission in "Travel by Wire" in 1937, though later writers rolled up the wire and simply broadcast from transmitter to receiver. The history of MT, from invention to galactic use in the far future, is followed in Harrison's *One Step from Earth* (1970).

Among the more interesting and oddball forms of transportation invented are the giant war-tanks that go boring and grinding away deep underground in Carter's "The Last Objective". On Jack Vance's *Big Planet* (1951) people roam the giant world in cars slung from ropes that loop from peak to peak □

CAPTION:

THIS SPREAD

TITLE:

GANT WHEELDRIVE

Space vice-Marshall Talian of the Capellan Shards Strategic Gaussi Space Fighter Force was something of an eccentric and renowned for his character and style. (See page 49, extreme right.) The Gant Wheeldrive vehicle was the Marshall's personal ground car and must have been the only remaining wheel-drive car in existence in actual use in the 25th Century. A genuine vintage it was actually powered by electromagnetic plasma motors and the illustration shown here, with the car seen from the rear, shows the plasma ejection nozzles. Woe betide anyone who stood too close to these nozzles when the Marshall put his foot down! The vehicle is stored in the PFCV 14 (see pages 16/17) and used on all independent travel across tough terrain.

# TIME MACHINES

THE TIME MACHINE is the magic carpet that makes all things possible. Inside this miraculous device—or even astride it—the push of a button can zip the traveller, and the reader back in time or ahead to the remote future. Like so much else in modern science fiction, we have the master himself, H.G. Wells, to thank for this handy invention. Eternity was pierced for the first time in 1895, in the book appropriately enough titled *The Time Machine*, and this is how the first-ever time voyage started: "*It was at ten o'clock to-day that the first of all Time Machines began its career. I gave it a last tap, tried all the screws again, put one more drop of oil on the quartz rod, and sat myself in the saddle . . . I took the starting lever in one hand and the stopping one in the other, pressed the first, and almost immediately the second. I seemed to reel . . .*"

All very nuts-and-boltsy, more like starting a Model-T Ford than using the electronic, force-field models of today. But none of the moderns has bettered Wells' description of rushing forward through time, ". . . night followed day like the flapping of a black wing." That flapping wing, and the "sun hopping swiftly across the sky" have been flapping and hopping ever since. Inside SF the subcategory of time travel has a well developed literature, with its own assumptions and accepted divisions.

And all of this despite the obvious fact that the concept of time travel itself is absolute nonsense.

Science fiction is a separate body of work, existing within the larger category of fantasy, itself a part of the modern novel as it is written in the west. Fantasy makes no attempt at all to be realistic or truthful, counting instead upon the willing reader's suspension of disbelief. Elves, gnomes, vampires and ''things too hideous to mention'' just don't exist. The reader knows this—yet enjoys stories about them. So while the inner, hardcore of SF is just a step away from reality with its submarines, flying ships, rockets, computers and Great Inventions, the outer fringes are at many times indistinguishable from the fantasy that surrounds them.

These are the reaches through which the time machines fly. But this is not to denigrate them in any way. Only the neo-Gernsbackians feel that every SF story must be tied firmly to science (if you can't patent it you can't write it). Time machines, impossible or not, perform a function vital to the literature. They are the vehicles that carry us into the future so we can examine the hardware and social organisations there in order to compare them to our own. This is a very different thing from the story set in the future and populated by locals. The time traveller is the contemporary reader who sees the utopias or dystopias of the future with a contemporaneous eye.

But to travel in time is to be presented with the temptation to alter events. Wells' Time Traveller could not resist going to the end of the Elloi and doing battle with the nasty Morlocks. Plenty of time travellers have been doing battle ever since, and an armoury of lethal weapons has been carried back-wards and forwards in time for both attack and defence. As early as 1938 Jack Williamson was writing about present events shaping the future-to-come in *The Legion of Time*. A year later L. Sprague deCamp had his hero working very hard to change the past in order to get a better future in *Lest Darkness Fall*. (The 'darkness' in the title is the Middle Ages which deCamp feels should never have occurred.) But once the ''alteration'' factor of time travel is considered we find that we have started a whole new ball game.

These alternate worlds are a great temptation to the writer-as-God and very hard to resist. Nor should they be resisted. At one time or another we have all said ''what if?'' What if we hadn't been in a certain spot at a certain time so that we would not have been involved in an accident? Or if this or that had happened we would have got the job. Daydreams are the stuff that literature is made of. What if the South had won the American Civil War? We would be living in a very different world, as Ward Moore pointed out in *Bring the Jubilee*. This sort of possibility generates the very SF theory of alternate possible worlds stretched out in infinite number. For if every event in the past could have happened differently—and the differences themselves varied from other differences—why then there might be in existence an

infinite number of alternate worlds. They would be branching and rebranching as more and more of the what-if events occurred. There is solid material here for the SF writers to explore for a goodly time. In addition the possible evil influences of some of the possible worlds calls for quick action by the Time Corps or other temporal policemen to go dashing around to stop the nasties from altering the past so much that we do not appear in the present.

Parallel worlds are a sub-category of alternate worlds. The theory goes like this; if there has been a branching in time in the past there will be a parallel world in existence very much like our own—though perhaps quite different. This parallel world, or worlds, exists in the same "time" as our own, though in a different universe or dimension or some such. Forever close by, forever inaccessible. Until the wonderful machine is invented. At first this is used as an inter-world one-way mirror or snooperscope to see what is happening in the other dimensions. Eventually it is used to open a door to the other world so hero and heroine can step through and have adventures. There is of course the reverse possibility, where the nasties in the other world slip through to cause trouble in ours. As early as 1917 in *Through the Dragon Glass* (perhaps owing more than a nod to Carroll's 1872 *Through the Looking Glass*) A. Merritt had his characters hopping through to explore the world beyond. All too often adventures in these worlds are more fantasy than science fiction, as in Zalazny's connected series beginning with *Nine Princes in Amber*, or in Moorcock's "multiverse" series of more than twenty linked novels. What the parallel world becomes is really up to the writer. Brian Aldiss wrote the definitive anti-novel, that is also an SF novel, in *Report on Probability A*.

A third category of subject matter arising out of the operation of the time machine is the time-paradox story. "What if I went back in time . . .

Herein lies the irresistible attraction of the time travel story. Scientific logic is thrown to the winds in exchange for all the things that make science fiction great. Colour, locale, action—and intellectual appeal. Despite Gernsback's patentable stories (and the Soviet SF's insistence on moral lessons) SF is basically a literature of entertainment. It continues to thrive because it contains more opportunities to entertain than the moribund detective story or the chap-flapping western. When you have seen one mysterious corpse, or a single, lonely rider against the sunset, you have seen them all. Not so SF where the limitations are only those of the author. If you think big you write big. A tip of the hat here to A.E. van Vogt whose grandness of concepts humble the writers who follow after him. Who else, other than the author of *Slan* and *The World of Null-A* would have written of the time traveller in "The Weapon Shops of Isher" who oscillates back and forth through time, picking up more "temporal energy" all the while, until he finally whips back to the distant past—where he explodes into the primary holocaust that starts the universe. Never had a hero gone out with a bigger bang.

The urge to rewrite history is a powerful one; we all cannot be as lucky as the Soviets who change it with every edition of their encyclopedia, or the Chinese who airbrush people out of photographs before they are reprinted. (George Orwell gave us the word for this process in his SF novel *1984*: doublethink.) However this process did not begin with the Sino-Soviets. It is old history. To a Bengali the Black Hole of Calcutta is a British propaganda story. A Dublin textbook of Irish history inserted into a Belfast classroom would cause instant book burning—and vice versa. When so much non-fiction turns out to be fiction who is to question the SF time machine that gives us another and closer look at variant history? I much prefer the SF version which is unashamedly fictional. Truth is hard enough to find at any time.

Theology has benefited a good deal from science fiction, although the theologians have not realised it yet. Although no SF writer has yet to be interested in meeting Mohammed as a small boy, a good many of them have craved a look in on Christ. But theology usually takes a beating in SF, and this theme is put paid to by Michael Moorcock where there is no Christ until the time traveller himself volunteers for the job.

It might be very well said that science fiction has a theology of its very own. The accepted theologies of the past were swept away by the advance of science, since no scientific discovery has ever supported any of the claims of the theologists. Geology has taken away the location of the underground Hell, while astronomy has revealed no Heaven above. With all of its philo- sophical and mechanical props removed, religion today is either nostalgic or soppily unspecific about an eternal Truth. Theologians, knowing only history, are untrained to deal with the discoveries and theories of contem- porary science; cosmology walks where theology never knew to tread.

Not so the science fiction writers. From Einstein's theory of the infinite yet curved universe, on through the big bang and steady state theories, SF writers have been marching side by side with the physicists and cosmo- logists. There is no theory so complex that some foolhardy writer won't turn into a story. (Witness the number of Black Hole stories—almost enough to fill a Black Hole.) The open-ended theology of SF, accepting everything but questioning everything, is a reflection of the best trends in social and scien- tific man.

This is not to say that the power of the irrational is not strong among SF writers and readers. With the strength of traditional religion diminished, the desire for instant salvation still exists. Witness the strength of the Salvation- by-Saucer cults down through the years, brought to a peak of enthusiasm by *Close Encounters of a Third Kind*. In SF we are not perfect—we just like to think we are ∎

CAPTION:

PAGES 100/101

TITLE:

PATERSON TD45

In the year 2611 on the planet Achamandura developments were completed surrounding the Paterson Time Dilatation theory and building began on the Paterson TD 1. Eighteen years later in 2629, after Paterson himself had retired, the Time Dilatation Federation set up specifically for time research built the TD 45 and succeeded in making the first uncorrected time trip without casualties.

By 2629 no less than 84 people had been lost in accidental time warps and 'correction trips' so that it was a relief to scientists involved in the Time Dilatation Federation to see their colleagues returned safely from a time trip into Achamanduran history, reaching a final date arrival point of 3339 (minus), all of five thousand nine hundred and sixty eight years into the past.

Full capacity and specification details are shown in the ISC sheets on pages 22/23.

The illustration on the previous pages was painted from video records taken

Continued next page

CAPTION:

THIS SPREAD

TITLE: LOVE MACHINE

The Lewis Tactil-Sensometer, employed here in relaxing and satisfying 1st Pilot Von Freyja (see also pages 48/9). The 'Love Machine' is used for male or female senior personnel from the Gaussi fighter crews after long battle routines.

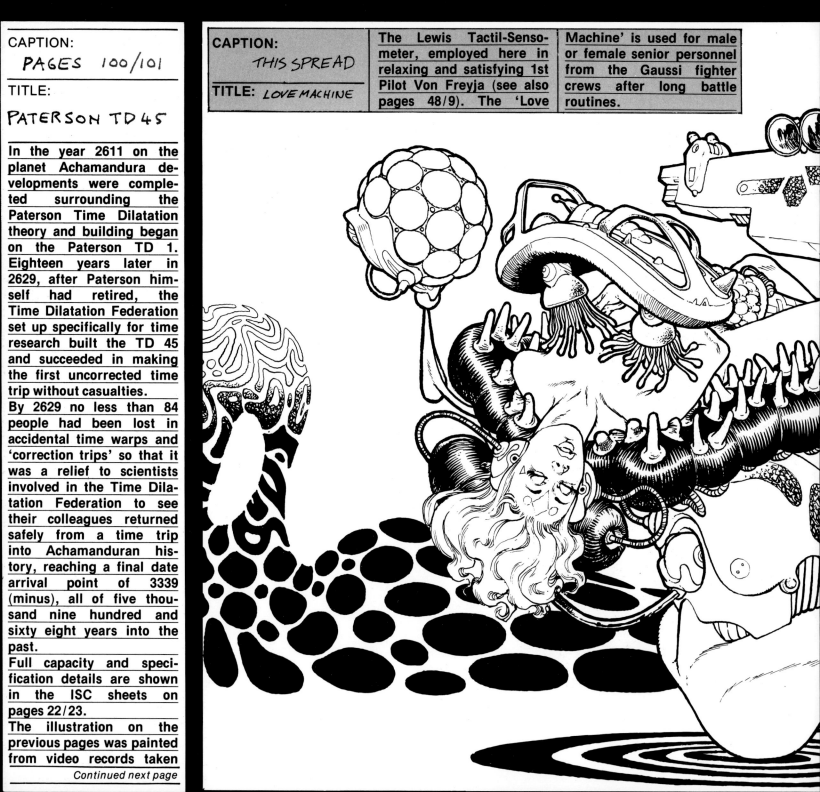

From previous page
by the TD 45 crew and the figure visible beneath the time machine is Dilatation Commander Patrick Orn. He can be seen surrounded by the 'Drop-time' halo effect, a device resulting from the change in his time position with relation to the surrounding environment. The 'Drop-time' halo also acted as a protection against time warp duplication.

CAPTION:

PAGES 104/105

TITLE:

P. M. MACHINE

The Perpetual Motion Machine, from the novel SUPERMALE by Alfred Jarry and illustrated here (following pages) by Russell Mills. Alfred Jarry's character William Elson creates a Perpetual Motion Food which is fed to cyclists who race a train along a 10,000 mile track and beat it. The five-man bicycle, standard 1920 racing model has no handle bars, fifteen millimetre tyres and moves, after being towed by a bullet-shaped car, at 120 kilometres per hour. The dwarf at the rear, named Bob Rumble, acts as a counterweight and served to increase or decrease the traction of the rear wheel.

# MOVIES

CAPTION:
PAGES 108/109

TITLE:
TSB 567/b

The TSB series was the biggest ever constructed during the history of the civilised Universe. The previous pages show an early illustration of one section of the computer which covered an entire planet named Tan-Major and the computer was named after the planet, being the Tan Series Banaconic relay 567/b. The letter 'b' was tagged on the end of the short specification name to denote that the TSB 567/b was the second TSB type, the first having been destroyed, effectively during the Division Wars by the Empire rebels, the Capellan Shards.

The Empire surrounding the Sirius Axis planets built the TSB to centralise their total administration and experimental functions. The administration sections of the computer were a back-up system which unitised and centralised all functions within the Empire and acted as a memory system for the Sirius history records. The experimental sections which took up the larger area of the series comprised a massive section devoted to what became

Continued next page

MOVIE: 2001: A SPACE ODYSSEY

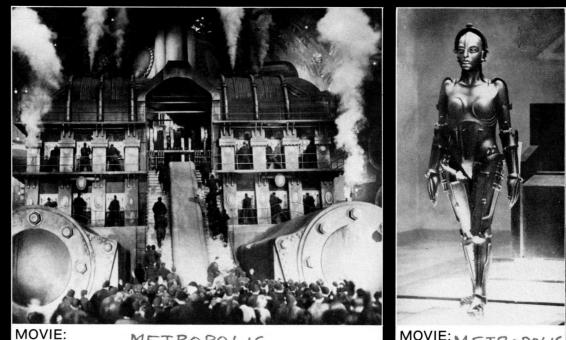

MOVIE: METROPOLIS

MOVIE: METROPOLIS

MOVIE: 20,000 LEAGUES UNDER THE SEA

*From previous page*

known as the Temporal Extrapolation Unit. This unit was used in the form of a psycho-historical analysis unit, gathering information from past trends and forming percentage analysis options which when translated into future trends could predict within a very sharp angle of accuracy exactly what could be expected in the future. During the Divison Wars the computer was largely out of action but during the latter half of the 25th century its functions formed a clearly useful aid to Empirical development.

MOVIE: SOLARIS

MOVIE: THINGS TO COME

CAPTION:

*RIGHT*

TITLE:

*SAND CREEPER*

**The Sand Creeper from the movie Star Wars, illustrated here by McQuarry. The Sand Creeper carried the Jawas across the deserts of Tatooine as they collected scrap metal, repaired old mechanical instruments and then sold them.**

TITLE: GLOSSARY

E-DATE: 2523.05.11

INDEX RETRIEVAL KEY: ☐☐O 8920

SECURITY STANCE: NIL

ACCESS: OPEN

SHEET NUMBER: 1

TOTAL: 2 SHEETS

DUPLICATION: U\L COPIES

THIS COPY NUMBER: 1

ASSIGNED TO: C.L. DENVIR

MICRO-FILE RECALL CODE: 01.437.3994

**Achamandura** — the only known 'walking city' planet. An inhabited planet within the territories of the Capellan Shards in the 25th century. SEE PAGE 64/5, explanation on PAGE 66.

**Animoid** — generic form of pseudo-animal used for guard duties, or pets on planets where biological animals are extinct.

**Battle Robot** — cybernetic devices involved usually in intergalactic wars, vary according to requirements. For examples SEE PAGES 23, 32/33, 38.

**BAVS** — Battle Area Vehicle Supremacy.

**Biotronic Missile Unit** — Battle Robot — SEE PAGES 32/33, 38.

**Byron Q Midgard** — Time traveller — SEE PAGES 50/51 and Newspaper report PAGES 116/7.

**Capellan Shards** — the rebellion forces in the 25th Century Division Wars — later to become the power behind the New Empire. SEE PAGE 12, 50/51.

**Celestian Cakewalker** — Hyper space travel — SEE PAGES 50/51.

**Charybdis** — Sirius Axis planet on outer access of old Empire where endemic cancer formed the SETcon operations which eventually forced 95% of the Charybdian population to become Mandroids and the entire planet to be isolated from the rest of the Universe. The Mandroid or Womandroid was 90% bionic and 10% human, usually with one eye and a human brain. SEE PAGES 37, 50/51 and Mandroid by Saul Dunn, published by Corgo Books, September 1978.

**Clever Metal** — a self repairing metal alloy-bio-conglomerate much used in Cybernetics and deep space military craft. SEE PAGES 10/11, 12, 22/23, 39.

**Cosmobender** — form of hyperspace travel — SEE PAGE 50.

**Cyberoid** — a worker robot used mostly by Capellans for farming and labouring duties — limited mental facilities. SEE PAGE 38.

**CYBORG** — tactical infantry unit, used for hand-to-hand battle requirements and espionage. Entirely biotic build — immense physical strength. SEE PAGES 38, 42.

**The Gant Wheeldrive** — Space vice-Marshall's personal land car — for full details SEE PAGE 92.

**Gaussi** — Fighter 724, 22/23, cover, 8/9, 10/11, 50/51. PFCV 14, 16/17, 22/23, 15. 10037 — central administrative planet of the Capellan Shards — page 12.

**Harold D'Algonquin Dazhbog** — space mercenary who worked extensively for Space vice-Marshall Talian in Divison Wars during the 25th century but who came to a sticky end at the hands of the enemy. For portrait see page 49, for biog. see PAGES 50/51.

**Hugo Le Griffe** — Space con man and well known author of the 25th century. For portrait SEE PAGE 48/49, for biog. SEE PAGE 50/51.

**Hyper-Space Troop Carrier** — largest form of light speed carrier vehicle employed in Gaussi command. SEE PAGES 21/2/3.

**IM4Pd Sentry Biot** — most commonly used cybernetic unit in the Gaussi command. Used mostly for guard duties, although carried extensive lab-grown brain units. For full details and visuals SEE PAGES 38/9, cover.

**INATMO** — in atmosphere travel.

**Island Three Space Colony** — theoretical NASA space plan to build complete space colony in orbit about Earth. For full details and visuals SEE PAGES 68/72.

**Janus** — one of the inner satellites of Saturn, terraformed in SGT 2210 — SEE PAGES 50/51.

**Koballium C-chip modules** — SEE PAGE 39.

**Mandroid** — 90% bionic, 10% human conglomerate built as a result of the SETcon operations on Charybdis. Process of conversion was developed to combat congenital cancer which threatened the sparse population of the planet. For full details and a visual of a womandroid SEE PAGES 38, 37.

**Niobe-Artemis Von Freyja** — Capellan 1st Pilot. Von Freyja was one of the most notorious pilots working in the Division Wars and became the first fighter pilot female to use the massive powers of the Gaussi fighter. She later became involved in more peaceful work on Charybdis. For full biog. and visual SEE PAGES 48/49, 50/51.

**Organic Disruptor** — A form of weaponry carried by military personnel and robots outside the Cybernetic Laws. Functions as a micro-cell disruptor — dematerialising the body by disbursement of the cells. SEE PAGE 39.

**Paterson Chronofractus-Disfuncto Miserere** — A form of time warp displacement — SEE PAGES 50/51 and 116/117.

**Photon Drive** — A form of space ship drive employing light in concentrated form.

**Plasto-Beryllomolybcarbactium** — hard wearing plastic-carbonate substance used in cybernetics and space technology. SEE PAGE 39 — Biot.

**Portamecks** __ lowly robot type with primitive B-chip modular expressed honeycomb brain, very high anti-grav capacity imparting immense weight-carrying strength but rather poor grav-correction ability which results upon accidental release of a big load in a portameck rocket-ting skywards and making large holes in roofs!

**Pseudo-Cyborg** — Most advanced robot-type ever developed. Capable of advanced self-perpetuating thought processes, with capabilities far beyond man's. Developed on Sirius Axis planets. For full details SEE PAGE 38.

**Quasi-demodiamond-plus** — the hardest substance known to man, with a surface strength capable of withstanding up to 8000 tons per square centimetre sustained pressure. Subsequently superseded by Superdense Polyconcrete. SEE PAGES 50/51.

**Ripple Rider** — Hyper space travel — SEE PAGES 50/51.

**SETcon** — Selected Enogenic Transfer conversion — the SETcon was the manner in which human beings on Charybdis were converted from 100% human to 90% bionic and 10% human having reached the age of 14 with the congenital cancer endemic on that planet.

**Sirius Axis** — Name of the Empirical forces involved in the 25th Century Division Wars. SEE PAGE 12.

**Sixth Sense Quasi-Psionic Esper 'Eye'** — A visual scanning system with 360° pick-up and 60% success rate on mental anticipation functions. Used mostly on IM4Pd Sentry Biots developed by the Capellan Shards and known as the 'Third Eye' because of its ESP capabilities. SEE PAGES 38, 39.

**Talian's Helmet** — SEE PAGES 48/49. Standard Capellan multi-function battle helmet. These helmets are 'grown' in a tank with molecular parameter measurements of the eventual wearer. The visor is made of quasi dermo-diamond plus (SEE GLOSSARY) with a light governed molecular alignment robocue. In effect this means that the polarisation gradient automatically adjusts with the light intensity. The

# MECHANISMO-FILE PRINTOUT

TITLE: GLOSSARY

E-DATE:

INDEX RETRIEVAL KEY:

SECURITY STANCE:

ACCESS:

SHEET NUMBER: 2

TOTAL: 2 SHEETS

DUPLICATION:

COPIES

THIS COPY NUMBER:

ASSIGNED TO:

MICRO-FILE RECALL CODE:

visor can withstand enormous impact, especially when at full polarisation. However at this stage the wearer would not be able to see through it so that a microcamera presents a video display in the front aspect on the inside of the helmet, adjustable from wide angle to 50 X zoom, incorporating infra-red and X-ray facilities. The helmet also contains a complete computer call-up facility. Through throat implanted microphones the wearer can use sub-speech (silent to all but the mics), and acquire any information required immediately. The relay can be received either by means of a hypersensitive sub-beam phone or visually on a head up display on the inside of the visor. In turn of course the experiences of the wearer are related to the computer. As a device to protect the helmet from falling into the wrong hands Space vice-Marshall Talian has fitted a surprise in the side of the helmet. He carries implanted in one of his molars a remote tap-code relay which, should the helmet be stolen triggers a vaporing 'Aldebaran Zuni-moth pupa', one of the most lethal life forms ever discovered, which he kept in a tiny hidden chamber just beneath the female demon emblem of the Shard forces on the left hand side of the helmet. Upon detonation this pupa would implode with incredible force destroying totally both the helmet and anyone tampering with it.

**Talian** — Space vice-Marshall Talian — legendary space commander in the Capellan Shards military. SEE PAGES 50/51.

**Tannochamber** — A reverberation chamber tied into computer functions, mostly used for voice simulation. SEE PAGE 39.

**Teedee Cannon** — A form of weaponry originally invented by the nation of French people on Old Earth in the 20th century and employing very low frequency noise emissions, tending to disrupt tissue and organs within the body.

**Thelxepeia Vrikshaka De 10** — Space prostitute grade one. The top rating for the professional lady with complete freedom of access to all inhabited planets, provided with private space vehicles and accommodation. For full details and visuals SEE PAGES 48/9/50/1.

**Transolar Lines** — Capellan Shards seconded from Earth's Solar System — SEE PAGES 50/51, 48/49.

**The Transolar Class 4 Clipper** — SEE PAGES 48/49. Dimensions: Length — 980 metres, Span — 721 metres, Height — 211 metres, Weight (empty) — 50,000 tonnes (extreme stress limit overload) — 93,000 tonnes. Performance: INATMO max speed — 1800 knots, running on two banks of governed hydra-twelve stellar fusion motors. EXATMO speeds max wer 3.25 DBVU (95,000 knots SR). FTL drive by a late Marque Rockwell 'Ripple Rider' (028/73 augmented) stabilised by a retrofitted ring of 160 anoramic preceptor foils.

**TSB 567/b** — The largest computer ever built, occupying an entire planet, built during the Division Wars and said to administer whole galactic systems. For full details see PAGES 106/7/8/9.

**White 'Port Security Guard'** — On Janus space port — SEE PAGES 50/51.

**Womandroid** — 90% bionic, 10% human conglomerate built from the SETcon operations on Charybdis. See Mandroid above and for visual and further details SEE PAGES 37/8.

**The X-On Core Latch Secrifact** — SHOWN ON PAGES 48/49 in the hands of 1st Pilot Niobe-Artemis Von Freyja, this piece of equipment displays holographically in the glowing yellow sphere the relevant information upon latch opening which in turn is governed by the 'key' which forms (1) a personal last minute identity coding of the presenter. (2) the passing of the personal eyeball print of the receiver and (3) a triangulated proximity response — automatic and pre-programmed — to two heavenly bodies, perhaps a laser gauged range estimate between the laser muzzle and the secrifact. In the 25th Century the X-on Core Latch was the most effective security device known.

THE

# GALACTIC TRIBUNE

**Published with The New York Times and The Washington Post**

DATE 2488 SGT 4/4 ——— Star-wide Newsprint reporting — up to the micro-second news. ——— 8 credits SFC

# TIME TRAVELLER TRACKED DOWN

by 'Buzz Tank' Billy

OUR WELL KNOWN feature writer has been at work recently researching one of the most interesting stories to turn up on the subject of time travel. It seems that one Byron Q Midgard is reappearing at intervals throughout the inhabited galaxies, caught up in what the experts term 'Chronofractus Disfuncto Miserere'. Readers will remember our report of the fated Paterson TD 39, one of the experimental time dilation craft developed before the successful TD 45 finally broke the time barriers and succeeded in returning without casualties.

Byron Q Midgard was Dilation Commander of the TD 39 and, during a trip back in Achamanduran history to a controllable point 1473 years before, he became enmeshed in a series of tragic technical mishaps while in 'Drop time'. As a result of these blunders he became permanently lodged in the Chronofractus effect. He vanished from space/time instantly, reappeared, confused and distressed in the same place five minutes later, stayed for a relieved twenty minutes and then vanished again.

Tracing his movements has proved problematic for Buzz Tank Billy but his efforts led him then through time and space to primeval Old Earth where the unfortunate Midgard apparently spent two years dodging the dinosaurs. From here he reappeared for half a Standard Hour on an unknown and unmapped planet where 'the very stones seemed to come after me' and 'the sky was a pulsating

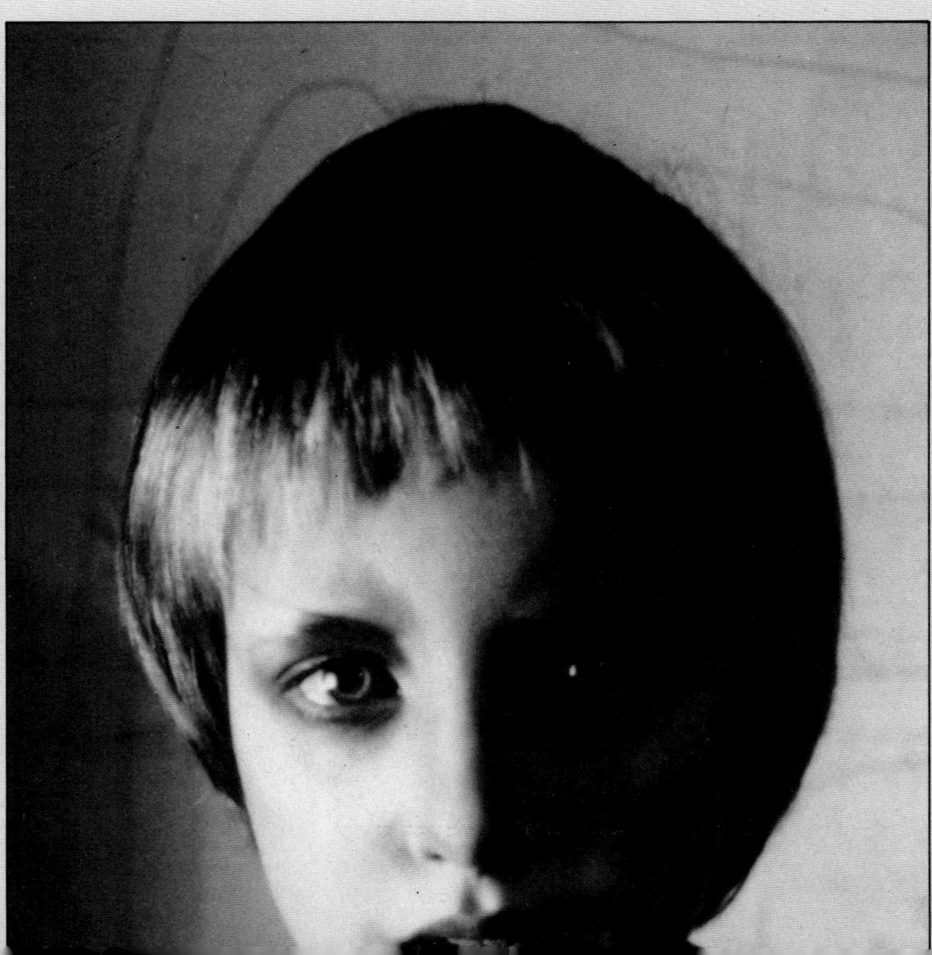

## STOP PRESS

JERRY CORNELIUS TELEPORTS IN TO ACHAMANDURA 23: 42.S.G.T. to receive 5.f.c. 7,000,000 for MOORCOCK MEMORIAL FUND.

NORTH SEA MONSTER—The largest moving object ever made, weighing over 601,000 tons

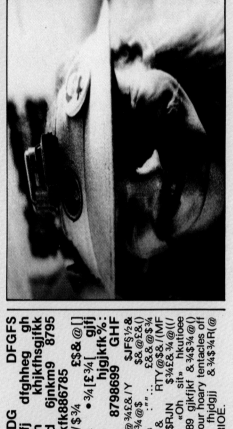

# THE DIVI WARS

**By Sdhywy Fphph**

OUR TRAVELLING correspondent as always at the centre of the action, sent up to the micro-second reports today for this edition from Abra-Minor where Axis 'Skid' launch attacks have rendered the local populace incapable of further defence. Capellan forces are said to be moving into orbit about Abra with eighty two Gaussi fighters and reports tell also of a Transolar arriving off limits, carrying two Battle Robots; the dreaded machines capable of laying landscapes waste.

The legendary Space vice-Marshall Talian is said to be passing through Sol system, arranging for large onslaughts into the heart of Sirius Axis territories using Earth seconded craft conversions and the well-known mercenary Harold D'Algonquin Dazhbog whom the Space Marshall has hired, is said to be preparing various plans for independent attacks on Axis outposts.

On Paliona VIII the FUEWE are hard at work undermining Axis Empirical efforts to calm the population by committing unpredictable acts of sabotage

Cont Page 27/Col 4

green,' states Midgard. This was followed by a ten year stretch in a reptilian cum humanoid society which accepted him readily but remains a complete mystery, then on to a frantic thirty five seconds on a planet whose sun was just going into nova. It seems that Midgard, despite this travel, does not age a second and his sanity and physical wellbeing appear little altered.

### Happy years

Following his near death on the nova planet he was swept into the welcoming arms of a pioneering woman on Proxima Centauri II where he spent 4½ happy years. Here, the woman whom Midgard has named Pasha bore him a son whom we have now been able to identify as Tinka-Mesh the sometime 'Blurred man of Proxima Centauri'.

It seems not to matter where Midgard goes, how hostile the environment or amenable the atmosphere he was always able to breathe the air. He always felt that he was breathing ordinary air which must have been coming to him through some kind of 'sub-space oxygen tube'.

linking him to his original place and time of departure.

He was once seen to stagger and clutch his throat during one appearance on Luna which may have been related to the accidental release of a quantity of 'noxistench' at the Paterson centre on Achamandura. Oxygen purity has now been maintained in that area in case the oxygen tube theory is correct.

### Doctors only theory

Only twice has he managed to stay stable in space-time for significantly longer than ten years, both times on Old Earth. Time Doctors have related this fact to a remarkable and untapped emotional facility in man relating to his evolutionary link with his ancestral home.

In one of his appearances Midgard was to spend a few moments on Janus to see the famous 'Biggest Window in the Universe' where an artist managed to capture his likeness (see pages 48/49, rear centre of picture). He vanished, leaving his clothes suspended in space in manform for a half second or so and confused a Portameck carrying the suitcase of a man not due to be born for over a hundred years. The Portameck is said to have dropped the heavy case and catapulted into the air to burst through the ceiling of the space port.

Midgard, in all his travels, found time to write a book on the subject, entitled *The Greatest Joke of All* the manuscript of which was found lying on an atom-tram seat on the planet Pustulus VII. Byron Q Midgard, we wish you Bon Voyage.

# HI-JACK RIP OFF

**Auto-Track Hi-jackers rip off Ucronion Faction.
Our Alien Reporter Jim (Paintbrush) Burns Reports.**

FGHDG    DFGFS
675hfj   dfghheg   gh
bfgdh    khjkfhsgjfkk
gfhgd    6jnkm9   8795
jfkjdkfk886785
* /@£/$¾    £$&@[]
[¼ ¼    •¾[£¾[   gjfj
&$-¾    hjgljkfk%:
" ± ]    8798699   GHF
$¾@¾£&/Y    $JF§½&
$&@£¾@$    $&@£&(\)
JHK¼    .'"·.:    £&&@$¾
RTY@&    RTY@$&//MF
£$&@$RJN    $¾£&¾@((/
GHJF   «Oh   sit»   hkutioee
i5847489 gjkfjkf &¾£¾@()
«Get your hoary tentacles off
me», fhjdgji &¾$¾R(@
IYUTRIOE.

## Index of Artists

**The author and the publishers would like to acknowledge and thank the following for use of material in this book:**

Young Artists, Jim Burns, Adrian Chesterman, Angus McKie, Brian Lewis, Bob Layzell, Terry Oakes, Alan Daniels, Russell Mills, Jennifer Eachus, Star Wars Corporation, Roy Coombes, Colin Hay, Mike Wilkes, Giger, Sphinx Verlag, Chris Achilleos, Bob Fowke.

Professor O'Neil for details of the 'Island Three' Space Colony from his book *The High Frontier: Human Colonies in Space.*

Artist Partners and the Carol Smith Literary Agency.

Jim Burns, Brian Lewis and Saul Dunn for their help in compiling the technical data.

The two illustrations on pages 44/5 were taken from the *Necronomicon* by Giger which will be published in the U.K. and U.S.A. in 1978 by Big O Publishing Limited.

The illustration by Chris Achilleos on pages 60/1 was taken from his anthology of art published this autumn in the U.K. by Dragon's World and in the U.S.A. by Simon & Shuster.

The movie pics on pages 110/1 are reproduced by courtesy of: *Metropolis* – U.F.A.; *Things to Come* – London Films; *20,000 Leagues Under the Sea* – Walt Disney Productions; *Solaris* – Mosfilm; *2001: A Space Odyssey* – M.G.M.